All about the Cocker Spaniel

By the same author

ALL ABOUT THE BOXER
ALL ABOUT THE STAFFORDSHIRE BULL TERRIER
THE STAFFORDSHIRE BULL TERRIER OWNER'S ENCYCLOPAEDIA
THE SPANIEL OWNER'S ENCYCLOPAEDIA

All about the Cocker Spaniel

JOHN F. GORDON

PELHAM BOOKS

First published in Great Britain by
PELHAM BOOKS LTD
27 Wrights Lane
London W8 5TZ
1971
Reprinted 1976
Revised Edition 1978
Second Revised Edition 1987

British Library Cataloguing in Publication Data
Gordon, John F.
    All about the cocker spaniel.—2nd rev.
    ed.
    1. Cocker spaniels
    I. Title
    636.7'52   SF429.C55
    ISBN 0–7207–1740–X

Typeset by Wilmaset, Birkenhead, Wirral
Printed in Great Britain by Butler & Tanner, Frome

Contents

Illustrations

Acknowledgements

I would like to thank Mrs E. S. Robertson ('Nostrebor'), Mr Ed. Simpson ('Coltrim'), honorary secretary of The Cocker Spaniel Club, and Mrs K. Baldwin ('Vailotest'), for their support. To The Kennel Club my thanks for the help and information always readily given. To the many Cocker fanciers and readers who have written to me over the years, may I assure them of the encouragement they have given.

Fees and Registration procedures of The Kennel Club are reproduced in this book by kind permission of The Kennel Club.

The photographs on pages 20, 21(a), 21(b), 34, 46, 62, 69, 88, 90, 91, 97, 99, 106 are by Roger Chambers; pages 19, 29, 39(b), 89, 107 by Gerwyn Gibbs; pages 39(a), 111(b) by Ann Roslin Williams; page 31 by Hartley; page 41 by Thomas Fall; page 111(a) by B. M. Mingay.

Preface

In writing this book, I have endeavoured to give a reasonably comprehensive coverage of the Cocker Spaniel's ancestry and the best way to breed, feed and care for him. This is a breed of considerable antiquity, but 'once upon a time' not so very long ago – less than eighty years in fact, the Cocker ran through a troublesome decade when his image was being overshadowed by other members of the Spaniel family. Rising out of mediocrity by the turn of the present century he has progressed substantially, hitting the high spots of public popularity and reigning supreme in the world of dogs. No dog could achieve such success without just cause. The Cocker's claim to fame is that he is a great dog in temperament, size, disposition and for general purpose work – all being factors which stand him in good stead. To those who own a Cocker these are assertions to be accepted without demur. To those about to buy one and having yet to enjoy the delights of Cocker ownership, appreciating the great companionship he can offer and the thrill of seeing him at work in the field – these are promises to be fulfilled.

I hope this monograph will enable Cocker folk to learn just a little more about their chosen breed – if so, then my work will have been more than worthwhile.

JOHN F. GORDON
ROMFORD

Preface to Revised Edition

It is pleasing to learn that a new edition of my book has been required. I have extended the section on the American Cocker Spaniel and the chapter on diseases as well as up-dating the Kennel Club regulations and making other minor amendments. The illustrations are new throughout.

The Cocker Spaniel, and now the attractive American Cocker Spaniel which has established itself well in the United Kingdom, thrive and multiply in the hearts and homes of fanciers everywhere. This important pair in the Spaniel family have set their pattern in the world of dogs and may they rise to even greater successes.

This seems a good opportunity to thank the many good folk in the breed who, having read the earlier editions, have written to express their appreciation.

J.F.G.
1987

1 Origins and History

What literature tells us

The Spaniel's history goes back at least five hundred years in England, probably an entire millennium as far as these islands are concerned if measured by the Ancient Welsh Laws codified by King Hywel Dda (Howell the Good) in 914 A.D. Then it seems, a Spaniel was held in high esteem:

> 'There are three kinds of animals:
> A beast; a dog; and a bird . . .
> There are three higher species of dogs:
> A tracker; a greyhound; and a spaniel.'

It was valued highly too, for when a Spaniel was stolen the thief would be fined 'three kine camlwrw' or three oxen or their value, sometimes more, according to the worth of the dog's services and the rank of his owner!

Undoubtedly, the Spaniel is a breed of great antiquity, but his origin is clouded with some mystery, due probably to the many centuries through which he has evolved and the lack of reliable data available to the student. However, some indication of his early history is revealed in the Metropolitan Museum of Arts, New York. There in the noted Cypriote collection is a small terra-cotta model, which in spite of its incompleteness is remarkably convincing as a Spaniel relic from that ancient civilisation. Phillips and Cane in their book *The Sporting Spaniel*, 1906 give the history of Denmark's chief honour the Order of the Elephant, said to perpetuate the memory of a Spaniel's loyalty for his master, a king deserted by his subjects. This is inscribed 'Wildbrat was Faithful'. The Order was in fact instituted during the reign of King Christian V (1670–1699).

In English literature, the first-known mention of the Spaniel by name was in the fourteenth century by Chaucer in his *Wif of Bathe's Prologue*. The lines are oft-quoted, but they serve still to prove the breed's early connections in Britain as well as its innate affection for an owner:

> 'She coveteth every man she may see,
> For as a Spaynel she wol on him lepe,
> Till she may finden some man hire to chepe.'

Perhaps a bawdy context and perhaps a Toy Spaniel too is envisaged, but Spaniels had not been divided into specific sorts and in those days even the small ones or Toys were frequently used in the field. In fact, there was a vast concourse of Spaniels, large and small – all more or less performing similar useful functions and all sprung from a common rootstock. It is believed that the original Spaniels were dogs of substance and fair size, probably similar in stamp to our present-day Springer Spaniels. It was not until about 1790 that Cockers and Springers were separated realistically, according to their function with game. In fact, the Springer was used for making game 'spring' from the ground and the Cocker was a 'wood*cock-er*', i.e. a dog to find woodcock and similar fowl in the undergrowth. The Cocker was then and is now, a smaller, more active variety and his development from the melting-pot of Spaniel stock came only gradually in the natural process of evolution and education.

In 1387 Chaucer's contemporary in France – Gaston de Foix, Vicomte de Béarn (1331–1391), chevalier and devotee of the Chase, alludes to the Spaniel in his great illuminated work *Miroir de Phébus*, 1387 or *Livre de Chasse*, as it is sometimes known. This was the outstanding work of the fourteenth century, having a tremendous effect on subsequent works on dogs. The fact that his immense hunting acreage abounded the Pyrenees lends some weight to contention that the Spaniel originated in Spain, although later T. H. Needham in *The Complete Sportsman*, 1817 and De Cherville refuted this. Nevertheless, de Foix's belief is generally accepted today.

Gaston's treatise served to provide Edward Plantagenet, Second Duke of York with much of his material to complete *The Master of Game*, written between 1406–1413 when the author was imprisoned in Pevensey Castle. It was the first sporting book written in English and served a good purpose because it brought Gaston de Foix's hunting experiences before those who might otherwise never have read them.

One reads:

'. . . Spaynels cometh from Spaine, notwithstanding that there be many in other countries' *and* '. . . a good Spaniel should not be too rough, but his tail should be rough' *and* 'they go before their master, running and wagging their tail and raise or start fowl . . .'

He goes on to extol the virtue of the breed when netting partridge and quail with the 'chien couchant' method, i.e. the 'sitting' or 'setting' posture system which Spaniels became famous for.

Virginia Woolf in her noted biography *Flush*, 1933 offers an interesting explanation to show how Spaniels could well have hailed from Spain. She refers to the historians who say that when the Carthaginians landed in that country (c. 238 B.C.) rabbits were to be found everywhere. The soldiery shouted 'Span! Span!', at the sight of them, this being their word for rabbits. The land became known and was eventually named *Hispania* or Rabbit-land and the dogs used by the natives to catch the rabbits called *Spaniels*! A colourful and attractive story no doubt which some might like to accept. Miss Woolf reports also that the Basques referred to the land as España, a word in their language signifying an edge or boundary. The dog coming from this region became known as a Spaniel; another likely explanation. We find too that in Old French, the word *espaigneul* is used in manuscripts which describe the Spanish Dog or Spaniel. In fact, there seems small doubt that the dog we know today originated in Spain. Were we able to travel back through time and inspect one of the originals we would probably have no difficulty in associating this early dog with one of the modern Spaniels, so strongly would the former's likeness have been transmitted through the many centuries of evolution. This, in spite of the manner in which the main rootstock has branched out to nine or more varieties of Spaniels which comprise the breed's family today.

The first actual listing of various breeds, although in simple form reminiscent of a school text book was *The Boke of St Albans*, 1486, originally *The Boke of Hauking and Huntyng*, written by Dame Juliana Berners, Prioress of Sopwell Nunnery. She names the breed 'Spanyel', but it is sufficient to establish the breed in England about five hundred years ago and this list remained unrevised for one hundred years after its publication.

In King Henry VIII's reign (1491–1547) Spaniels were popular in both the Toy and field varieties, although the Tudors made no apparent distinction between them. The household records of the palace show subsistence to one, Robin, Keeper of the King's Spaniels but it is not clear as to whether these were working dogs or 'Comforters' (described later by Caius as 'pretty playfellows' and obviously Toys). It is recorded however, that John Dudley, Duke of Northumberland (c. 1502–1553) was the first sportsman to train his Spaniels to hug the ground closely in order not to impede the bird-net as it was drawn up over and on to dog and quarry. It may be that he was the first Englishman to work thus with Spaniels, with the method of 'chien couchant' so clearly delineated in *The Master of Game* at the start of the previous century, but this claim seems unlikely.

A notable contribution to dogs with the written word was made by Dr Johannes Caius (or John Keyes, as he was known). A scholar and Physician-in-Chief to Queen Elizabeth I, also founder of Caius College, Cambridge he was the first to seriously divide the breeds. He attempted this at the request of his friend Conrad Gesner, the Swiss naturalist who wished to feature it in his monumental *Icones Animalium*, 1553. Caius produced his book *De Canibus Britannics* in 1570. It was in Latin and later Abraham Fleming, a student, translated it into English with his

Of Englishe Dogges, the Diversities, The Name, the Nature and the Properties, 1576. He refers to Caius, naming the Spaniel as Hispaniolus, revealing his belief as to Spain being the breed's birthplace. He says, and the words are Fleming's:

'The common sort of people call them all by one generall word, namely Spaniell – as though these kind of dogges cam originally and first of all out of Spaine. The most part of their skynnes are white, and if they be marked with any spottes, they are commonly red . . . othersome of them be reddishe and blackishe, but of that sorte there be but very few.'

The Boke of St Albans, already referred to, probably inspired Shakespeare's verse in *King Lear*, Act III, Scene VI which reads:

'Mastiff, greyhound, mongrel grim, hound or spaniel, brach or lym; or bob-tail tyke or trundle-tail,'

one of several references to the Spaniel among his plays.

Nicholas Cox in *The Gentleman's Recreation*, 1677 refers to the land Spaniel as a dog 'of good and nimble size, rather small than gross' and Phillips and Cane are responsible for telling us that Arcussia, a late sixteenth century writer, used black Spaniels with his falcons, the authors wondering whether these were the forerunners of modern blacks. In the same book, *The Sporting Spaniel*, 1906 they report from Taplin's *Sporting Dictionary and Rural Repository*, 1803 an interesting comment on the breed:

'Spaniel is the name of a dog which there are different kinds; and even these have been so repeatedly crossed that unless it is in the possession of sportsmen who have been careful in preserving the purity of the breed perfectly free from casual contamination, the well-bred genuine Cocking Spaniel is difficult to find. There are four different kinds of dogs passing under this denomination – the one larger than the other, much stronger in the bone, but with curly waves in the hair; and a small yellow-pied springing Spaniel (used in pheasant and cock shooting) whose hair is long, soft and delicately pliable, with ears of the same description, reaching, when extended, beyond the point of the nose. They are indefatigable in their exertions. From the time they are thrown off the pursuit of game, the tail is in a perpetual motion (called feathering) by the increased vibration of which an experienced sportsman knows when he gets nearer the object of attraction. The nearer he approaches it the more violent he becomes in his endeavours to succeed; tremulative whispers escape him as a matter of doubt; but the moment that doubt's dispelled, his clamorous raptures break forth in full confirmation of the gratification he receives. And this proclamation may be so firmly relied on (though in the midst of the thickest covert) that the happy owner may exultingly boast he is in the possession of one faithful domestic who never tells a lie.'

John Scott too, in his *Sportsman's Cabinet*, 1803 like other works of the same era says that Spaniels were evident in two distinct sizes. One was a larger variety, inclined naturally to 'spring' the game, the other, a smaller sort better suited for covert and woodcock shooting. The latter was the Cocker Spaniel in fact and described as 'a shorter, more compact form, a rounder head, shorter nose, ears long (and the longer the more admired) the limbs short and strong, the coat more inclined to curl than the springer's, is longer, particularly on the tail, which is generally truncated; colour liver and white, red, red and white, black and white, all liver colour, and not infrequently black with tanned legs and muzzle. . . .' He continues with '. . . the smallest Spaniels passing under the denomination of Cockers is that peculiar breed in possession and preservation of the Duke of Marlborough and his friends, where are invariably red and white with very long ears, short noses, and black eyes; they are excellent and indefatigable, being in great estimation with those sportsmen who can become possessed of the breed'. Of course, we know now that Marlborough did in fact conserve his variety under the name of his ducal seat – Blenheim and the breed became established there, becoming separated from the true Cocker Spaniel, although strongly influencing it by prior infiltration of its bloodlines. Blaine in his *Encyclopaedia of Rural Sports*, 1840, refers to the noble breed of Blenheims, crediting them with being 'zealous hunters in the field, but requiring much trouble to break' whereas Lord Rivers' noted black and white Cockers, on the other hand, '. . . turned out most excellent in the field and were shot to by us with less breaking than any others we ever remember'.

From the foregoing, it is clear that Spaniels as a family have passed through many centuries of evolution. They have branched out over the years into the many Spaniel varieties we know today. Undoubtedly, in the past the bloodlines have suffered adulteration, but this is a hazard that all breeds have had to bear – none more able to with equanimity than the anciently evolved Spaniel. Sufficient to say that out of the breed melting pot has come a variety of wonderful and useful forms, from which many have claimed the Cocker for their own particular love.

The Spaniel Club

This was the first breed club specialising in Spaniels. It was formed in 1885 by a body of experts and pioneers. The club's first function was to work on the various Standards of the breeds and Mr T. B. Bowers, a

Mrs E. S.
Robertson's
Nostrebor Nimbus

leading authority of the period did much to disperse the confusion which existed then, not only in pedigree matters, but with dogs' names and owners. From this gentleman's early efforts the first breed stud books were compiled.

In common with most breeds, the Spaniel suffered for many years the adverse effects of faddist breeding. Harmful trends such as the vogue for long backs and short legs were spoiling the breed; regressive features which included houndy heads and excess haw were rife and real lovers of the Spaniel became worried as to the breed's future. Important characteristics like temperament and workability were being overlooked and 'fancy' points, most of them useless, were taking precedence. A move was made by the Spaniel Club to arrange Field Trials, already proven advantageous to such breeds as the Setter and Pointer. However, the Spaniel Club, due to the difficulty in establishing a specific working standard for Spaniels was slow in organising an event. Another club was formed expressly for the purpose of arranging Field Trials, this being the Sporting Spaniel Society. Its first venture into Field Trials was held at Sutton Scarsdale (see section on Field Trials), which although successful was not so well supported as the Spaniel Club's own first Trials at Welbeck Abbey, home of the Duke of Portland. This was held on January 17th and 18th, 1900, two Stakes being run with the noted James Farrow ('Obo') and C. A. Phillips ('Rivington') adjudicating. This event was the forerunner of many similar events run by both clubs, all contributing substantially to the Spaniel's steadfastness in the field.

Cocker Spaniels up to this time had been forced, through no fault of their own, to take a 'back seat' in Spaniel affairs. This was due to them being regarded by many fanciers as too small for really hard work in the field apart from general uncertainty as to the breed's true function. These were the days when Field Spaniels and Clumbers were especially popular and whereas the former variety were bred to weights in excess of 25 lb, the Cocker was obliged to produce his type and uniformity at no more than 25 lb. These weight categories were rigidly enforced and Cocker progress suffered much because of it. Fortunately, the Spaniel Club abolished this arbitrary rule in 1901 and from this time the little dog began to prosper. Soon after the present century commenced, more and more Cockers could be seen in competition and the public started to show considerable interest in the breed. A club, the Cocker Spaniel Club was formed in 1902 to look after breed affairs and safeguard its interests. This task it has done conscientiously and effectively ever since. Since 1892 when the old Spaniel Club was instrumental in persuading The Kennel Club to recognise the Cocker as a specific variety, it has, apart from its first ten years in the 'melting pot' made rapid strides to the top plane in dogdom.

2 The Standard

The Cocker Spaniel

THE STANDARD
The Cocker Spaniel Standard (as published in 1986) is reproduced herewith by kind permission of The Kennel Club.

GENERAL APPEARANCE: Merry, sturdy, sporting; well balanced; compact; measuring approximately same from withers to ground as from withers to root of tail.

CHARACTERISTICS: Merry nature with ever-wagging tail shows a typical bustling movement, particularly when following scent, fearless of heavy cover.

TEMPERAMENT: Gentle and affectionate, yet full of life and exuberance.

HEAD AND SKULL: Square muzzle, with distinct stop set midway between tip of nose and occiput. Skull well developed, cleanly chiselled, neither too fine nor too coarse. Cheek bones not prominent. Nose sufficiently wide for acute scenting power.

EYES: Full, but not prominent. Dark brown or brown, never light, but in the case of liver, liver roan, and liver-and-white, dark hazel to harmonise with coat; with expression of intelligence and gentleness but wide awake, bright and merry; rims tight.

EARS: Lobular, set low on a level with eyes. Fine feathers extending to nose tip. Well clothed with long, straight, silky hair.

MOUTH: Jaws strong with a perfect, regular and complete scissor bite, i.e. Upper teeth closely overlapping lower teeth and set square to the jaws.

NECK: Moderate in length, muscular. Set neatly into fine sloping shoulders. Clean throat.

FOREQUARTERS: Shoulders sloping and fine. Legs well boned, straight, sufficiently short for concentrated power. Not too short to interfere with tremendous exertions expected from this grand, sporting dog.

BODY: Strong, compact. Chest well developed and brisket deep; neither too wide nor too narrow in front. Ribs well sprung. Loin short, wide with firm, level topline gently sloping downwards to tail from end of loin to set on of tail.

HINDQUARTERS: Wide, well rounded, very muscular. Legs well boned, good bend of stifle, short below hock allowing for plenty of drive.

FEET: Firm, thickly padded, cat-like.

TAIL: Set on slightly lower than line of back. Must be merry in action and carried level, never cocked up. Customarily docked but never too short to hide, nor too long to interfere with the incessant merry action when working.

GAIT/MOVEMENT: True through action with great drive, covering ground well.

COAT: Flat, silky in texture, never wiry or wavy, not too profuse and never curly. Well feathered forelegs, body and hindlegs above hocks.

COLOUR: Various. In self colours no white allowed except on chest.

SIZE: Height approximately: Dogs 39–41 cm ($15\frac{1}{2}$–16 in); Bitches 38–39 cm (15–$15\frac{1}{2}$ in). Weight approximately: 28–32 lb.

Mrs J. Schmidt's Sh. Ch. Matterhorn Montana

Mrs M. Snary's Sh.
Ch. Platonstown
Scooby Doo

FAULTS: Any departure from the foregoing points should be considered a fault and the seriousness with which the fault should be regarded should be in exact proportion to its degree.

NOTE: Male animals should have two apparently normal testicles fully descended into the scrotum.

THE STANDARD INTERPRETED

Although most Cocker enthusiasts visualise the perfect specimen in approximately similar light, it is seldom that two are found who interpret the breed Standard in exactly the same way. Unfortunately the Cocker with paragon virtues remains still unborn and although many superb specimens are seen on the show bench, the true supreme of breeding has

Miss P. Trotman's
Sh. Ch. Kavora
Charade

Clayforth and Peters'
Sh. Ch. Haradwaithe
Sorceress

yet to appear. The Cocker, as we have shown, is an ancient breed – it marches nearer to perfection than most breeds we know today but there remains a distance to go before some breeder can claim he has a perfect specimen. Even when this occurs, no doubt the claimant will have his antagonists!

To learn the Standard properly, it is necessary to refer to a living specimen whose worth is freely acknowledged in the breed, and whose abidement by the points of the Standard has been confirmed and approved by a number of reputable championship show judges. Study the Standard in conjunction with this dog at every opportunity – find out just what the people who formulated the document were thinking about when they wrote it. Remember this is a word-picture of the perfect specimen and forms the basis on which modern Cocker breeding has been built. Obviously, it cannot possibly conjure up the same picture in different minds, even were it more precise and detailed in its form. Assuming that you had never seen a Cocker Spaniel before – would you ever be able to mould a mental picture of one just by reading these few terse sentences? Clearly, you need to see the living flesh in ideal Cocker form *first*, coupled with a written description of the dog which is factual and well phrased so that it can be understood and used to perpetuate in breeding the desired Cocker form. Thus, in reading the Standard we start with:

GENERAL APPEARANCE: This infers that the Cocker's appearance must be pleasing; that it will impress you and attract your attention. His good demeanour, outline, balance, size, sound action and merry disposition must be in evidence. A lot can be learned in the initial assessment of a dog and as the eye becomes more practised it will select at once any physical failings, type deficiency and signs of imbalance. An impressive Cocker will radiate not only style and good type, but display boldly the 'blue blood' of his fine pedigree breeding, just as surely as a dog lacking all these requisites will never look the part.

Movement plays an important rôle in an assessment of general appearance. Standing, a dog may well look a picture of excellence, all his physical components being of a high order, but when he starts to move it may become clear that the overall mould of his structure lacks coordination. His movement will be affected adversely, for in truth, such a dog is basically unsound and the linkage or coupling of his limbs especially is at fault.

The Standard does not mention Balance, but it is important. In fact, good balance should be evident from all angles. Most people look for it in a dog's profile, i.e. his outline. It should be sought too in his front, his rear and even three-quarters face on. It must be evident as he moves fore and aft and when seen alongside. A sound Cocker moves soundly with a flowing gait, typical of his breed. Soundness is another essential unmentioned in the Standard, but it is of *paramount* significance in the field of pedigree dog breeding. A dog, no matter how impressive he is in physical points when standing, is quite worthless as a show dog and breeding prospect if he lacks soundness. This can be either induced or inherited. For instance, a dog might fall from a height and break his leg. From the moment of accident until restoration to normal use the damaged leg will render its owner unsound. This is induced or temporary unsoundness. On the other hand, if a dog inherits straight stifles making his gait stilted and thereby affecting his stamina as a working dog, then he is permanently unsound and nothing can be done about it. A vicious dog should be considered unsound, for this is not a tendency expected in Cockers. Any structural weakness makes for unsoundness. It is said that a dog out of condition is unsound; this is true although perhaps pedantic and the main forms of unsoundness come from structural, physical and temperamental imperfections. The rule for deciding unsoundness, whether temporary or permanent, revolves around the effect of the disability upon the Cocker's usefulness. If he is affected in even a minor way then the dog concerned is unsound. If it is of a temporary nature then the dog can be used for breeding with no known hazards, but if the unsoundness has been passed down by his parents then he will never prove an asset to any conscientious breeder.

In conclusion, no Cocker can hope for full marks in this section if he lacks Condition. A dull, felted coat, lacking the silky finish and bloom one expects to find in a healthy dog would brand him at once as an ill-cared-for specimen of little consequence. In effect, to shine in the stakes for General Appearance, a dog must look *good*!

HEAD and SKULL: The Cocker Spaniel's headpiece when in its ideal form is a beautifully sculpted feature. As with all breeds, a good head attracts more attention and admiration than any other part of the body for it is the dog's dominant point. The skull and brow should be well-formed and developed and the length of head should be made up with a pleasing proportion between the skull and length of muzzle. Balance in head is just as important as body balance. No matter from what angle the head is examined the main sections, viz: skull, muzzle and jaw must coordinate in pleasing fashion. No abrupt definition should exist in its chiselled lines, all the contours being stylishly moulded with no bumpiness at the cheeks. Nevertheless, the stop should be distinct, even in the puppy stage. This is particularly important today as there seems a trend towards flatness where this indentation should exist just in front of the eyes. Should this be so, it is to be deplored, being quite wrong as a breeding policy.

EYES and EARS: These must be included in any assessment which incorporates the head and skull. Expression varies from breed to breed but Cocker Spaniel expression is unique with its mixture of gentleness, honesty and intelligence. However, eye shape can deflect this attractive aspect into something of lesser appeal. If the eyes are too small a 'varminty' glint can be produced; too large and prominent and the expression will become vapid, both outlooks which are untypical. Light eyes and eyes which are too dark in colour will militate against true expression and an undue display of haw is objectionable too. Eye colour is allowed to vary a little with different coat colours – the Standard tells us that one can harmonise with the other. Unfortunately, opinions as to what is harmonious and what is not, vary too, individuals being what they are, so not too much licence should be allowed in this matter. Positioning of the eyes plays an important part in the maintenance of correct outlook and the fancier as he becomes more experienced will soon learn to recognise bad eye emplacement by the poor aspect it bestows on the dog.

The ears should extend from just where they are set-on to the head at or slightly lower than eye level, across the cheeks to the tip of the nose. This provides an ideal length and although they should be well furnished with rich, silky hair, the featherings should not be exaggerated – merely adequate. The ears should lay down well from the skull without thickness where they set on, for this will give an unwanted impression of coarseness in the skull.

NECK: The neck of a Cocker is a point of beauty; most artists over the centuries seizing upon it when expressing their work in the Spaniel field. It needs to be strongly constructed and so well set on to well-laid back shoulders as to effectively control head carriage and provide an easy linkage which will contribute towards the dog's good movement.

FOREQUARTERS: The Cocker's forequarters must be strong to allow easy front action, and be so constructed as to stand up to hard work in the field. The important feature in any dog required to work and maintain long hours over rough ground are well laid back shoulder blades. Without sloping shoulders the dog's action will be stilted, causing him to be tired quickly and lack resilience to pressure and jarring shocks. The Cocker's front should be straight with ample bone right down to the feet and not 'fluted' below the knee, which will suggest weakness at this point. The front should not be too wide as this will not only impair the dog's pleasing balance, but detract from the free and untiring style of his gait. Conversely, the front must not be tight, indicative of shoulder emplacement which is inflexible due to the inferior angle made by the shoulder blade (scapula) and upper arm bone (humerus). This poor articulation of the two bones will produce an untypical, mincing movement. The chest *must* be deep and well developed with *moderate* width, accompanied with good depth of brisket, that part of the body which lies below the chest and between the front legs. The lower line of the chest, when viewing the dog's entire outline in profile, should pass through the upper section of point of elbow.

BODY: A Cocker Spaniel needs well-sprung barrel ribs if he is to do his job properly. These need to be sufficiently roomy and elastic to house the dog's heart and lungs and allow for their protection and expansion when in maximum use. The ribs must be well laid back, with ample spring notably towards the back end of the chest in order to provide utmost capacity with length, for the efficient working of the lungs.

The back should be strong, compact and generally well-knit, all parts flowing into a pleasing whole. If however, a Cocker is too short in back he will sacrifice elegance and certainly find his working ability will lack flexibility. Exaggeration in any physical department becomes a fault and is therefore to be deplored as much as a deficiency. The topline of the back should be level, but curved off a little over the croup to where the tail sets on. This does not mean that the backline should drop abruptly to the set-on, as this would entail weakness in that region.

HINDQUARTERS: A working dog like the Cocker needs great propelling machinery in order that he can perform his tasks quickly, efficiently and untiringly. This means he must be well endowed with long musculation on legs and buttocks. Bumpy muscles are strong and good for short-term work, but they lack the stamina of those which are long, hard and well-toned. With such development, properly distributed and with particular emphasis upon the musculature of the first and second thighs coupled with the bend of stifle, a dog can work for hours with no discomfort. Straight stifles are caused by straight instead of well bent articulation of the two (first and second) thigh bones. It is a common fault in many breeds and any Cocker with straight stifles cannot move as a Cocker should and can be considered unsound. Further, his hind angulation will be at fault and as the hock is too high, the dog's stride is rendered untypical. Viewed from behind, the skeleton has to be straight and true, but the actual muscle development which surmounts it provides a more bolstered appearance. Under no circumstance should there be any signs of cow-hocks (where the points of hocks turn in to each other, thereby throwing out the feet) or in-toes, where the hocks are thrown out away from each other due to the feet being turned in. Such defects can be induced, when they are features of temporary unsoundness; often however, they are inherited and Cockers with such faults as well as other structural defects are of little use to a discerning breeder.

FEET: These should be compact and well rounded, not too large, yet in line with the bone structure of the limbs. A Cocker with a loose, open foot will soon tire at work and the pads, unless strong and well cushioned, will become sore. Plenty of exercise will ensure that the nails are kept short, hard ground work being best to achieve this. If for any reason a Cocker cannot be exercised, his nails should be trimmed as required. A dog bad on his feet is unable to move well, no matter how good he is in other departments as a show dog.

TAIL: As the Standard says, this is 'characteristic of blue blood in all varieties of the Spaniel family' and it has been shown many times that a first-class specimen whose tail did not wag 'merrily' as he moved away from the judge can be faulted drastically. As with all 'special desiderata' and most breeds have them, a Cocker's tail action, while vitally important to him, should not represent the 'be-all and end-all' of his worth. Among the varieties of Spaniels, the Cocker is allowed a *slightly* higher action than the others, but this does not mean he can carry it cocked up. It should be carried out and roughly in parallel line with the topline of the back. Unfortunately, a young show dog or a good specimen with little liking for the show ring will perform badly with his tail purely for temperamental reasons. A judge will usually know how to discriminate in such matters, making allowances for it in much the same way as he might concede certain failings in other departments. Nevertheless, it is useful to breed your Cockers with good, 'merry' tails. This saves a lot of worry and frustration if you contemplate the show ring for your dogs. In the field, a good working dog's tail action should be incessant; this keeping his master informed as to progress in the covert, acting as a signal, according to the tempo of its vibrations. Because of this use, also for the reason that a good tail contributes so much towards breed character, it must not be docked too short.

COAT: The Cocker's coat, more or less in common with other members of the Spaniel family must be flat and glossy. This conforms not only to the Standard's requirements, but is a fair sign of the individual's good health and condition. The texture should be silky with no suggestion of waviness or wiry finish. It needs to be close and weather resistant, but avoid letting it become too profuse, while maintaining an adequate garb of feathering.

COLOURING: The colour range permitted by the Standard is wide. However, white feet and white on the chest are generally ostracised, although some concession is allowed in respect of the latter – at least, by the Standard's wording, where the *self-colours* (or solids) are concerned. Desirable colours in the breed can be maintained by selective breeding, which to a large extent can dispense with mis-markings. Care should be taken when assessing parti-colours and tri-colours as compared with whole-coloured stock. Sometimes markings are 'unfortunate' in that they detract optically from a dog's true worth, suggesting perhaps a physical weakness, even a fault where none exists. The experienced judge will not be deceived of course, but occasionally ringside critics become victims of this optical trap.

WEIGHT and SIZE: The Standard asks for Cocker weight to be '*about 25–28 lb*', which allows some scope for breeders to produce good Cockers which will not be precluded from major awards merely because they exceed the higher figure by a pound or two. The essential factor in breeding to size and weight is to produce a dog which apart from having adequate bone substance with type and quality, is pleasingly balanced. Often, when breeds have a fairly flexible weights section, the best specimens will fall into a category extending beyond the upper limit, often as much as by four to five pounds. It has been proved, to the breed's disadvantage in the past, that it is unrealistic to set an inflexible limit of weight, thereby rejecting completely all specimens, however good, if they exceed that weight. Nevertheless, the elasticity of the present-day Standard's weight clause must not be abused. The Cocker has to be a small, busy and merry dog, able to penetrate deep covert, inaccessible to a larger variety. He must be maintained thus.

MOVEMENT: Few breed Standards detail the movement expected of their dogs and Cockers have no guidance in this respect. A Cocker's action should be studied as the dog comes towards you, walks away and as observed from the side. Simply, it should be easy, brisk and confident, the forefeet stepping out in positive fashion, the tread being neither wide nor narrow. The elbows should be well in at the sides without any evidence of tightness at the shoulders. Proppy or stilted action will indicate poor shoulder emplacement and a paddling or weaving movement of the feet can arise from looseness in the same upper frontal region. The action should be reasonably springy, confirming strength and suppleness in the pasterns. Seen from behind, the Cocker's movement should again be neither wide nor narrow, some inclination towards width being perhaps preferable. Good effect is achieved when the Cocker's hind legs move in parallel to each other throughout their length, i.e. from hip to foot, flexing well at the points of stifle and hock. One with loose hip joints or with bad articulation of the stifle joint is often cow-hocked, i.e. with points of hocks turning in to each other. The hocks should be well flexed as the dog moves away, contributing all the time to the Cocker's typical stride and rhythm. Seen from the side, the Cocker should move with his head held up well, the neck well arched and flowing into the body via the withers. The dog's topline should be level and firm, rounding off slightly where the tail is set on to the body. The tail itself, the Cocker's 'hall-mark' should be in constant action while carried out from the stern, rather lower yet in parallel line with the back.

TYPE

Type is not easy to define, but can be said an absolute essential to the Cocker Spaniel if he is to approximate to or represent his breed in an ideal form, as laid down by his breed Standard. A Cocker who has type, while not necessarily perfect throughout, has many features which can be claimed as typical and desirable. A Cocker lacking type can perhaps have one or two good and typical features, but is overall only a fair example of his breed. It should be realised that whereas a dog can 'teem' with type, he can be totally unsound! In effect, his physical features or components, while each is individually excellent as an example of the specified section of the Cocker breed Standard, do not fuse together in sound and pleasing form, their articulation or linkage being faulty. Such a specimen might well look good standing, but reveal his inherent weaknesses when moved. He is of no value to any self-respecting breeding programme as such faults of structural linkage are transmittable.

The American Cocker Spaniel

The American Cocker Spaniel is assuming such importance in the world of pedigree dogs that no book on the Cocker can be complete without reference to him.[1]

The American Cocker Spaniel was introduced to England's show rings by Yvonne Knapper and her imported Sh. Ch. and American Champion Kaplar's Kwik Step to Sundust was the top gundog in England in 1984 and ranked as ninth top dog all breeds. The breed is a strong contender in Gundog Group at Championshiop Shows and its great ability in the field promises well for an important future in the United Kingdom.

The American Cocker Spaniel is immensely popular in the United States where it is known as the Cocker Spaniel. In 1983 and 1984 more than ninety thousand were registered by the American Kennel Club and the breed led in registrations again in 1985. This is a nightmare situation for serious and dedicated breeders as it brings with it many unscrupulous breeders whose main interest is in making a profit with total disregard for temperament or health problems.

Descended from the union of a Sussex Spaniel sire and a Field Spaniel dam many American Cockers in the British show rings can trace their ancestry directly back to early origins in the late 19th century. He differs from his English cousin in size, the ideal height for males being fifteen inches at the shoulders and fourteen inches the ideal for bitches. The American Cocker's head has a rounded skull with a clean, deep stop; the eyes are larger than those of the English Cocker, and the muzzle is square and deep.

In spite of the modern American Cocker Spaniel's profuse coat his working ability has not been lost. Working American Cockers have their coats trimmed much shorter than those exhibited in the show rings. In

[1] I am indebted to Mrs Yvonne Knapper (formerly Weyland) of the world-famous 'Sundust' prefix for supplying the up-to-date information in this chapter on this now very popular breed.

Gibbs

American Cocker
Spaniel: Mr and Mrs
D. Cristofoli's
Semsox Ghostbuster

England there are two full champions and though not many are worked with the gun there are several working well for their owners on private estates. On one such estate two American Cockers work amongst the owner's Labradors and Springers.

While excelling as a show dog the American Cocker is a delightful companion. He is a very outgoing little dog and is more adaptable than his English cousin. Although he is the smallest member of the Gundog

Group do not be fooled by his size. He is full of energy and fun, and although the American seems to need less exercise than the English Cocker do not think he dislikes it; he loves to go for long walks and will adapt himself to his owner's liking for exercise.

Exhibitors of the American Cocker Spaniel become experts in caring for the breed's heavy coats but careful and regular grooming is a necessity for all American Cockers. Owners of companion dogs have a serious responsibility to take their pets to an approved professional canine beautician for regular bathing and trimming every six to eight weeks. The preparation of show dogs is quite intricate and involves expert hand stripping of the back coat.

Since their introduction as show dogs in England the American Cocker has prospered well (see Appendix 2) and risen in popularity in many European countries as well as in Australia and New Zealand. In Sweden an American Cocker must obtain a Field Certificate before it can be awarded a champion's title and when Yvonne Knapper judged the breed at Skokloston in 1986 two full champions and one international champion were entered, underlining the fact that the American Cocker can work if given the opportunity. In Sweden they begin their training at the tender age of eight weeks!

The American Cocker Spaniel makes its presence felt in the show rings of every country where it appears and is renowned for its Best in Show wins at all breed shows. The breed's latest success in winning through to the position of top gundog, all breeds, was in Australia where this was achieved in 1985.

The Kennel Club recognise him as a pure breed and put on offer 34 sets of Challenge Certificates for 1985. Already, this transatlantic cousin of our own Cocker has made an impact on the British showbench world with a number of major wins. His breed Standard is remarkable for its detail, something which will appeal to the discerning breeders here who are now kennelling the American Cocker Spaniel and intend to campaign him to successful heights.

THE STANDARD OF THE AMERICAN COCKER SPANIEL
(Reproduced with the kind permission of The Kennel Club)
GENERAL APPEARANCE: Serviceable looking dog with refined chiselled head, strong, well boned legs, well up at the shoulder, compact sturdy body, wide muscular quarters, well balanced.

CHARACTERISTICS: Merry, free, sound, keen to work.

TEMPERAMENT: Equable with no suggestion of timidity.

HEAD and SKULL: Well developed and rounded, neither flat nor domed. Eyebrows and stop clearly defined. Median line distinctly marked to rather more than half-way up crown. Area surrounding eye socket well chiselled. Distance from tip of nose to stop approximately one-half

American Cocker Spaniel: Mrs Y. Knapper's Sh. Ch. Thanks Be Be from Sundust

distance from stop up over crown to base of skull. Muzzle broad, deep, square, even jaws. Nose well developed. Nostrils black in black-and-tans, black or brown in buffs, browns, browns-and-tans, roans and parti-colours.

MOUTH: Jaws strong with a perfect, regular and complete scissor bite, i.e. upper teeth closely overlapping lower teeth and set square to the jaws.

EYES: Eyeballs round, full and looking directly forward. Shape of eye-rims gives a slightly almond appearance. Neither weak nor goggled. Expression intelligent, alert, soft and appealing. Colour of iris dark brown to black in blacks, black-and-tans, buffs and creams, and in the darker shades of parti-colours and roans. In reds and browns, dark hazel; in parti-colours and roans of lighter shades, not lighter than hazel; the darker the better.

EARS: Lobular, set on line no higher than lower part of eyes, feather fine and extending to nostrils, well clothed with long silk, straight or wavy hair.

NECK: Long, muscular and free from throatiness. Rising strongly and slightly arched.

FOREQUARTERS: Shoulders deep, clean-cut and sloping without pro-trusion, so set that upper points of withers at an angle permitting wide spring of ribs. Forelegs straight, strongly boned and muscular, set close to body well under scapulae. Elbows well let down, turning neither in nor out. Pasterns short and strong.

BODY: Height at withers approximating length from withers to set on of tail. Chest deep. Lowest point no higher than elbows, front sufficiently wide for adequate heart and lung space, yet not so wide as to interfere with straight forward movement of forelegs. Ribs deep and well sprung throughout. Body short in couplings and flank, with depth at flank somewhat less than at last rib. Back strong, sloping evenly and slightly downwards from withers to set of tail. Hips wide with quarters well rounded and muscular. Body appearing short, compact and firmly knit together, giving impression of strength. Never appearing long and low.

HINDQUARTERS: Strongly boned, muscled with good angulation at stifle and powerful, clearly defined thighs. Stifle joint strong without slippage. Hocks strong, well let down; when viewed from behind, hindlegs parallel when in motion or at rest.

FEET: Compact, not spreading, round and firm, with deep, strong, tough pads and hair between toes; facing truly forward.

TAIL: Customarily docked to three-fifths of tail. Set on and carried on a line with top line of back, or slightly higher, never straight up and never so low as to indicate timidity. When dog in motion merry tail action.

GAIT/MOVEMENT: Co-ordinated, smooth and effortless, covering ground well.

COAT: On head, short and fine; on body, medium length, with enough under coating to give protection. Ears, chest, abdomen and legs well feathered, but not so excessive as to hide body lines or impede movement and function as a sporting dog. Texture most important. Coat silky, flat or slightly wavy. Excessive coat, curly, woolly or cotton texture undesirable.

COLOUR: Blacks jet black; shadings of brown or liver in sheen of coat undesirable. Black-and-tan and brown-and-tan (classified under solid colours) having definite tan markings on jet black or brown body. Tan markings distinct and plainly visible and colour of tan may be from lightest cream to darkest red colour. Amount of tan marking restricted to ten per cent or less of colour of specimen; tan markings in excess of ten per cent undesirable. Tan markings not readily visible in ring or absence of tan markings in any of specified locations undesirable. Tan markings located as follows:

(1) A clear spot over each eye.
(2) On sides of muzzle and on cheeks.
(3) On underside of ears.
(4) On all feet and legs.
(5) Under tail.
(6) On chest, optional, presence or absence permissible.

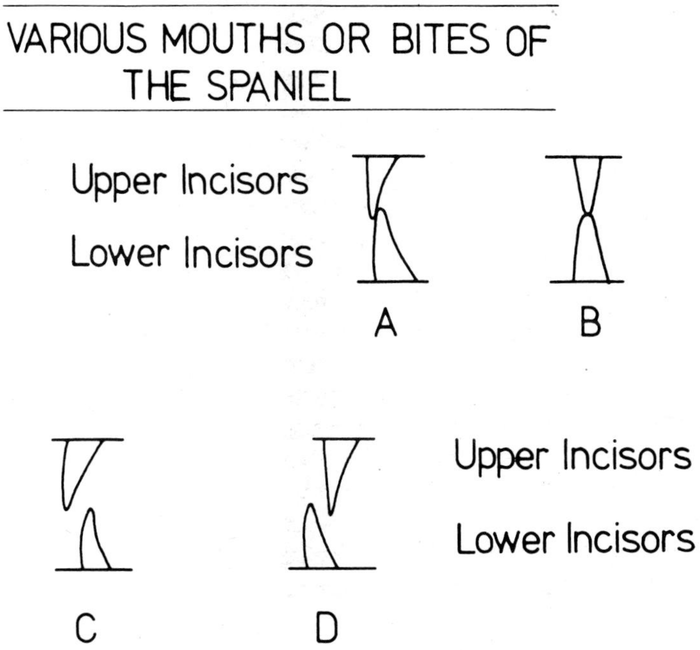

VARIOUS MOUTHS OR BITES OF THE SPANIEL

Upper Incisors

Lower Incisors

A   B

C   D

Upper Incisors

Lower Incisors

FIG. I. DIAGRAMMATIC SKETCHES SHOWING THE VARIOUS MOUTHS OR BITES
OF THE SPANIEL

(A) *The correct mouth. The upper incisors fit closely over and upon the lower incisors,
allowing a clean scissor bite.*

(B) *The 'flush' mouth. The upper and lower incisors meet tip to tip, allowing an even
although wearing bite. Not a satisfactory mouth.*

(C) *The overshot mouth. The upper incisors protrude beyond the lower incisors with
space between them. In the exaggerated form known as 'pig-jaw'.*

(D) *The undershot mouth. The lower incisors project beyond the upper incisors with
space between them. Regarded as a show fault.*

Tan on muzzle which extends upwards and over joints highly
undesirable. Any solid colour other than black or uniform shades.
Lighter colouring of feathering permissible. In all above solid colours a
small amount of white on chest and throat while not desirable,
permissible, but white in any other location highly undesirable.

Parti-colours. Two or more definite colours appearing in clearly
defined markings essential. Primary colour which is ninety per cent or
more highly undesirable; secondary colour or colours which are limited
solely to one location also highly undesirable. Roans are classified as
parti-colours and may be of any of usual roaning patterns. Tri-colours,

A. and A. Webster's
Sh. Ch. Asquanne's
Genevieve

any of above colours combined with tan markings. Tan markings preferably located in same pattern as for black-and-tan.

SIZE: Ideal height: (The word approximate leaves too much to chance)

Dogs: 36.25–38.75 cm (14½–15½ in)

Bitches: 33.75–36.25 cm (13½–14½ in)

FAULTS: Any departure from the foregoing points should be considered a fault and the seriousness with which the fault should be regarded should be in exact proportion to its degree.

NOTE: Male animals should have two apparently normal testicles fully descended into the scrotum.

3 Breeding

WHEN TO BREED

Most people owning a nice-looking Cocker Spaniel bitch will wish to breed from her at least once and a litter or two during the early years of her life is well worth considering. Not only can pedigree dog breeding offer an owner tremendous interest, probably even some financial reward, but to the younger members of the family it can provide a useful education. The best time to arrange for a bitch to be mated is when she is at her second heat or season, providing this occurs when she is not less than fourteen months of age. If for any reason, the heat in question occurs a month or two earlier than this, then leave her alone until the next season breaks. Should her intervals of heat continue irregularly, it might be wise to have her examined by your veterinary surgeon who will know what to do in order to have her ready for the planned mating.

The breeding life of a Cocker Spaniel can extend up to ten years, even more in unusual cases, but the average Cocker bitch should not be bred from after six years of age. This assumes she has had a previous litter or two and whelped them easily and reared them well too. No Cocker bitch should be mated for the first time beyond the age of three and a half years; to do so could prove hazardous, although not necessarily if her strain is noted for its good whelping ability, when a further six months extension can be granted giving her a chance to prove her procreative powers. In any case, a mature Cocker in whelp should always be referred to your veterinary surgeon who will agree to stand by on the expected whelping date to give assistance if required. Note that because a bitch, especially one of advanced years, has what appears to be a normal season, this does not mean she will definitely conceive, even with a reliable stud dog's efforts. These days, the incidence of false heats and 'misses' (when a mated bitch fails to conceive) becomes more common. No-one knows quite why this is; probably it is due to some chemical deficiency occasioned by the domestic dog's way of modern living. A bitch so affected does not shed ova at the time of her oestrum, so there is nothing there for the male to fertilise at mating time.

In a way, it is unfair to put the rigours of nursing upon an older bitch. If you intend to breed, breed from a good, sound, well set up yearling. She will tackle the job of producing and nursing her first litter with enthusiasm and no doubt produce something worthwhile for you if you have been careful in your selection of the sire. In any case, if you have a good Cocker you will help the breed along by increasing its population, providing you strive to produce stock which is at least as good as, preferably better than the parents. This might appear a very difficult task, especially if one or both the parents are champions! However, your duty to the breed will be done by ensuring that both members of the proposed union were compatible in type, style, temperament, health, soundness and pedigree before putting them together. This condition is no more than a simple duty to your chosen breed and if you are successful it will prove most inspiring in the satisfaction it gives.

Before contemplating a union make sure your bitch is fit, and apart from the normal meaning of fitness which encompasses soundness (both body and temperamental) as well as health and bloom, it is essential that she carries no excess weight. A fat bitch is likely to 'miss' or at least have a difficult whelping, maybe with considerable veterinary expense. Even worse, it is not unknown for mortality to occur when the bitch is obese and ill prepared for the duties of motherhood; this in itself being a peril showing how important it is to ensure the Cocker is in good supple trim at all times.

Methods of breeding

LINE-BREEDING

This is the more generally used system of breeding, used by expert and novice alike. It is a fairly slow method of getting the end result, but it has the advantage that it is safe, even in the hands of the novice, any little miscalculation shown in the result of one litter being reasonably easy to correct in the next. Because of this, a strain's progress is unlikely to be halted for long. Line-breeding, refers to the unions of:

> Grandson to Grandam
> Grandsire to Granddaughter
> Nephew to Aunt
> Uncle to Niece
> Cousin to Cousin

In effect, this is the mating of dog and bitch with similar blood-lines allowing one ancestor to appear twice in the previous three generations, although not within the last two. It is most important that the animals used in this breeding plan (as indeed in all progressive breeding) should be selected with care and not only look like each other, but conform to the stringent requirements of breed type, temperament, health and soundness. Failure to take care can result in the introduction of less desirable features becoming rooted and difficult to eradicate.

IN-BREEDING

In this system the mating pair are close relatives, viz:

Sire to Daughter
Son to Dam
Brother to Sister

revealing the need for delicate handling of any breeding programme so planned. One ill-conceived mating can easily contribute to the ruination of a long-maintained strain. Strictly speaking, in-breeding is for the expert, even the geneticist perhaps, but in any hands it is risky. Designed to 'fix' good, therefore desirable breed points in a strain, it can just as easily produce faults, hitherto latent, in double measure. Because of this, it is clear that only the best-looking purest breed stock be employed in in-breeding. Even more important than in line-breeding, the stock must be selected with maximum care, ensuring type, health, soundness and temperament in full measure. Obviously, this is breeding for the true expert only and even he may well find himself non-plussed after producing several generations of in-bred stock to know how far he dare proceed further into the system. In fact, many having reached such an *impasse* are forced to turn to an out-cross for their strain's salvation.

OUT-CROSSING

Sometimes when a strain has been subjected to excessive in-breeding over a number of generations it becomes exhausted or *effete*. It becomes necessary at this stage to introduce or inject new blood into the strain, primarily to improve its health and constitution, while preserving if possible its excellent type. This means employing an out-cross from strong and totally unrelated stock; such a dog being at least similar in type to the strain he is required to improve. The fact that his ancestry is unlikely to have anything in common with the in-bred strain is all to the good, providing the mating produces stock with desirable characteristics rather than inferior points. This is a risk the breeder has to take when he uses an out-cross; it is worthwhile taking it for he seemingly has little choice if his strain has become dilute. It is not unknown for champions to be bred in this way, although such dogs are really no more than chance good ones, which while good in themselves may not carry latently the characteristics which go in the blood and bone of the pure strain of one parental type. The clever breeder when seeking a useful out-cross tries to find a dog which is somewhere linked well back in his pedigree with the purer strain's strongest line.

DEVELOPING A STRAIN

It is not unusual to find many Cocker breeders of long standing still without their own acknowledged strain. Actually, if you have embraced a breed it is nice to plan for and produce your own distinct stock, but to be of any worth a strain must produce Cockers distinct in type and their own special markings perhaps with every generation. Of course, it goes without saying that the features shown must be desirable ones as far as the Cocker Spaniel breed Standard is concerned. When you have fixed these points in your strain and the strain becomes known by your name or prefix when seen in the show ring or on the bench you will have 'arrived'.

Success cannot be achieved merely by the simple process of using regardless the breed's most fashionable stud dogs. Some of these dogs while good to look at can well have little to offer from their breeding background. Always use the dog who while of the same type as your bitch is able to offer some useful bloodline link from his pedigree breeding. Further, and this is most important, make sure that he has produced good stock, offspring that you yourself would like to own. Never waste time with untried, unproven stud dogs however attractive; let others use these and watch results without cost to yourself. Always fix virtues first; this is more important than toiling to eradicate minor faults. Once you have stamped a head or ears or some other wanted virtue on your stock you can deal with the faults later as the opportunity arises.

Study of pedigree

Pedigree *is* important, but it is only as good as the dog himself. Conversely, the dog is only as good as his pedigree. It is not much use boasting you have a wonderful pedigree for the Cocker you own if the dog has clearly no worth as a breed specimen. Likewise if you own a handsome Cocker Spaniel and his pedigree reveals that he has sprung from nondescript breeding, he can be of little use to you or others in the breeding field. Such a dog is a 'sport' or chance good one and is unlikely to reproduce his own good looks even when mated with great care and selectivity. This is why some superb looking specimens never make their mark in the breeding field whereas a less handsome stud dog might well produce a number of champions in his issue.

When you contemplate a breeding programme, try and track down the dogs whose names appear in the two pedigrees representing the mating pair you hope to use. This will prove difficult for some of the dogs involved will be dead while others are living in obscurity. However, collate as much data as you can, using the good services of The Kennel Club's registration department, another source being well-versed breed experts, usually with long memories and plenty of records. Old show catalogues are helpful too; in fact, you will find many of the actual show dogs involved were exhibited in one or more of the regional breed clubs.

E. and J. Simpson's
Lochdene Ping Pong
of Coltrim

K. and M. Rees'
Teifi Black Sparkle

The secretaries of these will undoubtedly prove helpful if approached in the right manner. At least, try and get information on the *important* ancestors – some of these might conceivably have been responsible for several lines, many of which will have tapered away and become extinct perhaps due to faulty and imprudent selection. However, where an important and strong line has been developed and solidly maintained, this can and should be 'tapped' to your own advantage. Never hesitate to draft out on paper all the distinctly successful genealogical breed lines relevant to your planned mating. You will find this system both illuminating and instructive when preparing the groundwork of a project which with a little luck could produce a champion for you!

Selecting your stock

The conscientious and ambitious breeder selects his breeding stock with the greatest care, insisting on absolute soundness in all departments – skeletal, physical and mental. No shelly animals can be permitted into the well planned programme; likewise nervous and unreliable dogs must be discarded, however good the individuals are in other respects. The male dog should teem with masculinity as well as type, just as the female parent-to-be must be well endowed with femininity and type. Not only the male's pedigree breeding, but his physical appearance should suggest that he is able to complement or remedy any existing imperfections in the bitch and conversely the same applies. Pedigree, as we have shown in a previous section, must be understood. Each parent's ancestry should be pictured in your mind as clearly as your data will allow. In this way, you will have some ideas as to the sort of breed background you are putting into the melting pot, so to speak, with this planned union. Select as far as possible parents who have already proved their worth in the breeding field. A good sire whose pre-potency has already been irrefutably established is worth half-a-dozen better lookers about whose progeny nothing is known.

CHOOSING THE BITCH

Do not be misled into believing that a mediocre bitch will necessarily make a good brood bitch. Mediocrity in itself is a fault and easily perpetuated; on the other hand, if she is without glaring faults and is well-bred she could produce useful and typical stock when mated selectively to the right stud dog. All puppies are born drawing their type and points (both good and bad) from their dam as well as their sire. Some people would have you believe that the only parent to consider in breeding is the dog – the dam, they say, contributes only a very small part of her worth to the issue. It is a fact that most of the big breeding and show winning kennels owe their success to and have been built on

Mrs M. Robinson's
Craigleith bitches

the worth of one foundation bitch. This bitch will have been one of great type and soundness, possessing ample substance and merit both apparent and inherent. More important, she will have had the ability to pass on these worthwhile attributes. Such a bitch is an acquisition to any kennel and if you can get such a one to start yours, you are fortunate indeed. The obvious place to seek for her is among the members of a successful bitch family, she herself being as good a Cocker as you can find at the price you can afford to pay.

It is important that she be roomy, which means in body she is sturdy with a generous rib-cage, which is both barrelled and extending well back, allowing ample lung and heart room. There should be good width of pelvis with well developed hindquarters. She must have no glaring faults such as an undershot jaw, yellow eye, cow-hocks, loose shoulders, straight stifles and elbows which throw out – for these are readily transmittable to her young. She should have a good Cocker head and carry herself sweetly enough to be described as a good mover, using her well set tail in the desired way. Temperamentally, she must be sound – nervousness and viciousness, should they exist being often inherited tendencies. If she has had puppies previously, you are fortunate in that you can seek out some of her earlier sons and daughters and assess their worth, always bearing in mind the type of dog used with her to produce them. Enquire whether the bitch mothered her puppies well. A poor mother at whelping and nursing times will set a flaw in any otherwise well conceived breeding scheme, quite apart from the fact that her daughters can inherit the tendency and become bad mothers in their turn.

Some breeders like their bitches to be a little 'doggy', i.e. to have a dash of masculinity (with substance) about them. This applies especially where the head is concerned for they feel that a doggy-headed dam will guarantee good heads in her progeny or at least will compensate for a side lacking in head qualities. This form of thinking is wrong; not only does it imply negative qualities in the stock to be used, but it countenances the use of exaggerated features, which do not always work to a breeder's advantage. This is because an exaggeration is a fault in just the same way as is a deficiency. Therefore, always select parents whose required good features are *normal* and typical of their sex.

The best age to buy a brood bitch is when she is about twenty months old and has had one litter, this successfully. At this age you can see what you are buying and her past is so recent that you can check easily enough on her history. She is young enough to reveal her true character and disposition, to come under the wing of your ownership without qualms and offer you her lifetime of work and companionship, which in turn should be repaid with kindness, consideration, affection and proper care.

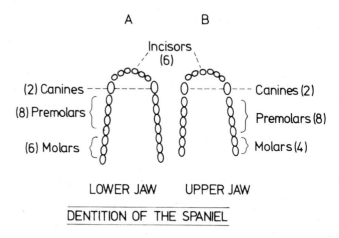

DENTITION OF THE SPANIEL

A. Lower Jaw =   6 Incisors   B. Upper Jaw =   6 Incisors
                 2 Canines   2 Canines
                 14 Molars   12 Molars
                 ───   ───
                 22   20

FIG. 2. DIAGRAMMATIC SKETCH TO SHOW THE DENTITION OF THE SPANIEL

INSIDE THE MOUTH

When buying an adult Cocker it is prudent to check not only the condition of the animal's teeth, but to verify that it has a full set of natural teeth in both upper and lower jaws. Brown-stained teeth, usually referred to as 'Distemper'-teeth, indicate that the dog was a victim of one of the high-fever virus diseases during puppyhood. It is common in dogs never immunised when young and the enamel will be found discoloured and badly impaired. This will have been caused either by the high fever experienced or some metabolic disturbance associated with the particular infection. When such teeth are noted, check to see if the Cocker has been impedimented in any way by Chorea, which is similar to St Vitus' Dance, or a like aftermath of disease such as Distemper.

Domestic dogs have usually 42 teeth, 20 in the upper jaw, 22 in the lower jaw. Occasionally, individuals have more, but from front to rear it is normal to find (in the upper jaw) six incisors, two canines, eight premolars and four molars. In the lower jaw, six incisors, two canines, eight premolars and six molars. A puppy starts off with permanent molars in the hinder part of its mouth and retains these, whereas the premolars are erupted over the conventional six month period and replaced with permanent 'second' teeth. The carnassial tooth, which is the largest cheek premolar (see fourth premolar in diagram) is later replaced by a permanent tooth. This is in the upper jaw and the corresponding member in the lower jaw is actually the first molar, which remains with the dog all his life. The canines are the largest, their roots being deeply buried more than double the length of the part to be seen. Keep a close eye for teeth which are found loose or missing. This may be due to accident or be of genetic origin, and probably not easy to determine the actual cause.

PUPPY OR ADULT?

It is probably better to buy your Cocker Spaniel while it is still a small puppy, although if you are anxious to commence showing and breeding, you will be tempted to get a bitch whose worth and promise you can evaluate without too much guesswork being involved, who is over one year old and more or less ready to breed from. Regarding the price you will have to pay, this depends largely of course on the quality you contemplate, also from whom you are buying the dog. Puppies today are fairly expensive and show prospects are at a premium, and a really top class adult (if you can get one) costs a lot, for most owners of such stock have little desire to sell it and will have to be tempted by financial considerations.

When you buy you must insist on absolute assurance as to the dog's physical, temperamental and productive soundness. Many advanced puppies and older dogs are put on the market because they have proved unsuitable in some way to their original owners. You must make sure that you do not buy one of these for the dog will probably prove just as useless to you. When you buy an older dog always pay with a post-dated cheque, subject to agreement on this point with the vendor. This will allow you a week or ten days approval and in this time you should be able to ensure that the animal is sound temperamentally and without vice. Should she show unreliability or any chronic unpleasant feature, then do not complete the sale and return her to the seller. Of course, you cannot determine her breeding worth until you have actually produced from her, although it is sometimes possible to check with her owner as to whether he has bred from her or attempted to breed from her. View reluctant comment on the subject with some doubt and make every effort to safeguard your own interests – there can be no recompense once the deal has been finalised. You should find out if the dog is house-clean. An ill-trained or sluttish adult bitch can take all the joy out of ownership. Many who have spent most of their early lives in the kennel, where cleanliness at night is not so important as it is in the home, never become fully house-trained. A bitch like this becomes unpleasant and irritating to have around and an owner may wish that he had invested instead in a small puppy which apart from a few innocuous puddles at first could be house-trained in a very short time. Further, some older dogs do not change their owners and homes easily. They fret, remain upset and aggrieved and never seem to entirely associate themselves to a new owner, his home and family, whereas a three month old puppy settles in happily within a day or so and can be quickly got used to the geography of the home and trained to its routine. Cases will vary with the individuals concerned, but generally speaking these are the main factors involved when deciding between a puppy and an adult. However, it must be born in mind that buying a puppy straight from the nest with exhibiting in mind can be no more than a gamble. No-one can possibly assess the show future of such a baby – even the greatest expert, in spite of what he might claim. Too many things can go wrong in the later months although a distinct strain might have been evolved and maintained for years from which good ones are readily recognisable from mediocre ones when only a few weeks old. Attributes in such young stock can be discerned, but not necessarily taken for granted or considered permanent. Show merits can be assessed only in dogs which are *at least* six months old, at least with any degree of certainty.

DOG OR BITCH?
The answer to this question depends largely on your purpose in buying a Cocker, quite apart from field work, which subject this book does not attempt to cover. If it is for breeding, then clearly your choice must be a female. A bitch can fulfil your needs in the show ring too if she is good

enough; even if she is not at least you can breed with her to a good and well selected dog in order to improve on her own type and points in the subsequent progeny. From her litter in due course, you can retain a bitch puppy, carrying on the strain and striving to improve all the time as you breed. You will find that most Cocker fanciers who are one-dog owners prefer a bitch in the home rather than a male. The old days when bitches were an embarrassment have gone. Today you can employ veterinary deodorants, some to be taken orally, others to be applied externally. These will cloak the bitch's menstrual scent which excites and attracts the male dog. Further, a female is less likely to wander abroad – unlike a dog who at ten months of age is liable to get an urge to seek out bitches for himself, sometimes travelling miles away from his home in the quest. The female too is instinctively a good guard (dogs are sometimes lazy in this respect) and will give prompt warning if she thinks the security of her 'nest' (in this case your home) is threatened. You may find her more loyal and affectionate too as well as a delightful companion – all points which may encourage you to decide in her favour when making your purchase. It has been found that many one-time male-dog owners transfer their affections to a bitch when they make their second purchase; and those who have got used to owning bitches seldom lean towards a male when the time comes to buy another.

BUYING A PUPPY

The main consideration when buying any form of livestock is *soundness* and *good health*. These essentials encompass the Cocker's structure, his physical points and his temperament. Possessing them compensates a dog for any deficiencies he may have in type and points of the Standard. Poor type is not something you would call in your veterinary surgeon to improve, whereas a dog with constitutional weaknesses and constantly recurring bouts of ill-health will prove always a worry and an expense. Thus, if you are buying for companionship, type is much less important than health and soundness, but if you intend to show and breed you must have health, soundness as well as type and quality.

There are plenty of Cocker Spaniel puppies to be had, as a rule, and a nearby source of supply will invariably be found in the appropriate sale and stud columns of the dog papers. It is safe enough to buy from a distant kennel however, providing the breeder is reputable or you have been recommended to him. Even so, when some distance is involved always insist on the dog coming on approval against your remittance, the understanding being that you can return the dog if you find it unsuitable or not as described when it arrives. In the event of a return this should be effected within twenty-four hours and your remittance should then be returned intact unless you have made some special arrangements as to whom should defray carriage and costs. Failing a personal arrangement

Trio of 3-month old
puppies

like this, the dog papers run a deposit scheme intended to protect buyers
and sellers, a small fee being charged for the service. No buyer should
expect to be free to return livestock after a protracted period unless with
full consent of the owner and the dog or puppy involved should be
properly fed and attended while awaiting transit.

If you can make a personal visit to the kennel which has puppies for
sale it is of course much better than to buy unseen, especially if you can
make your choice from an entire litter. Nothing is worse when buying a
puppy to find your selection restricted to a solitary puppy, the inference
being that all the best have already been sold! This is not always the case
however, for many breeders dispose of their poorer puppies first,
retaining the prime and more saleable puppies to the end. Assuming that
you have a litter of six puppies to select from you will find some at once
eliminated depending on whether you want a dog or a bitch. An odd one
or two will follow suit as you discard them according to your personal
preference as to their colour and/or markings and disposition. If the
breeder is a well-known and reputable man he will almost certainly
discuss breed points on the remainder with you, if you request it. Very
often show kennels, knowing they cannot possibly handle all their
promising puppies themselves are only too pleased to put potential
winners into the hands of exhibition-keen novices. A well campaigned
and successful dog with the kennel prefix on his name can advertise their
breeding very effectively in this way.

However, if you prefer to depend entirely upon your own judgement, thinking that perhaps you have 'an eye' for a good one, then it is worthwhile to go ahead. Firstly, dismiss as unwanted any weedy, too-small puppy, also the one who is undershot, nervous or mismarked. A puppy showing distinct faults at this age will never be worth anything to you or to Cocker posterity. You will now have to consider the remaining puppies. Keep an eye on the good-looking youngster who is lively and fearless in his approach. He should have a good dark eye imparting intelligence and gentleness. Expression is important even in a dog so young and should have every consideration when assessing the worth of a puppy who will probably spend his life with you.

The next task (and in this you may need expert comment to guide you), is to evaluate the puppy in relation to the various points of the Cocker Spaniel breed Standard. Look for bone and substance in any case. Bone which is too coarse may suggest a puppy which will go oversize. That which is thin and 'fluted' indicates skimpy skeletal construction and although bone can sometimes be improved with calcium and good feeding any real bolstering is doubtful. Stand the puppy up on a table at chest level. Examine his front and hind limbs. The front should be straight, the forelegs parallel and the bone good right down to the feet. There should be no weakening at the pasterns and the feet should not be big, flat and splayed but nice and compact. The shoulders must slope nicely, the neck showing already some beauty in its line and reach. The hind legs should be firm and parallel when viewed from behind, there being no indication of cow-hocks or similar weaknesses. Examine the head, probably the most important feature, and not very easy to assess in a puppy, for at ten weeks of age nothing is really distinct and definite enough to study with a view to its future development. However, refinement and classical line should be present. Over-development of the skull with bumpy prominences at the low level of the ears should be viewed with suspicion as they suggest coarseness in later life. The ears should be set on at or just below eye level and when stretched out the tips should extend to the puppy's nose. The stop should be defined and the muzzle nicely squared off. The mouth should be level, i.e. with the upper incisors resting over and upon the lower incisors with no gap between the two rows of teeth. The merest exaggeration of this formation is permitted – in fact, some breeders like to find it in a small puppy as it allows for the lower jaw to develop a little as the second teeth form and with maturity the mouth remains correct.

The puppy when viewed from the side should be square in outline, well put together and nicely balanced. The tail must be set on in the right position, i.e. just below the level of the backline with which it should run parallel. A slightly down-carried tail can be normal at this age, just as some brash puppies will boast high tail carriage while teething; it does not matter so long as the set-on is right. Examine the underparts for healthy, well-toned skin. Acne-like spots might mean the puppy has worms or external parasites. The breeder should be queried on these matters although it is unlikely to be anything but a harmless puppy-rash. If the puppy is a male check that both testicles have descended into the scrotum; cryporchids are today not worth owning, although in young puppies the entirety is often difficult to confirm, the second testicle dropping later. Run your fingers through the puppy's coat, assessing its quality and gloss as well as the texture of the skin below. No white should be found on the chest of any self-coloured coat, although a few white hairs are usually ignored. Nevertheless if you can avoid buying a solid coloured dog so marked you should do so.

Apart from the importance of checking for good movement in your puppy by watching him run around, also back and forth to you, try and be there when he passes a motion. Its consistency should be firm, rather like porridge and a healthy colour. A loose motion need not indicate sickness, but it should be pointed out to the vendor and providing you are quite satisfied that the youngster is in good health and take him home, he should be put on to a milky diet for the next twenty-four hours. This will soon clear up what is probably no more than a simple puppy tummy-upset. However, keep a close watch on a dog's motions always; they are a good guide as to the pattern of his health. Enquire of the breeder how he has fed the puppy and secure a detailed diet sheet. The same form of feeding should be followed for a day or so after you get your puppy home, but it can be gradually weaned over to your own way of feeding. Most puppies go off their food soon after reaching their new home. This is due to finding themselves alone, the strangeness of their surroundings and change of food. If you can do anything to make their rehabilitation easier you should do so, as it will hasten their progress. Ask when your puppy was last wormed; most breeders worm their puppies between five and six weeks of age and for a second time a month later, but if the second worming has not yet been done it will become your responsibility. There are a number of excellent vermifuges and vermicides on the market. Probably the best one to use is the one the breeder himself used. The puppy will not thrive properly until these unpleasant parasites have been entirely dispersed.

Once you have decided on the puppy you want, it is advisable to pick him up, pay for him and go without further ado! If you vacillate you may well be tempted to change your mind and take one of the others – to your later regret, perhaps. The breeder should have all the puppy's documents ready for you – Pedigree, Kennel Club Registration Card, signed Transfer Form, not forgetting the Diet Sheet. Payment should be made and a proper receipt obtained for the money.

SELECTING THE SIRE

Too many people select a stud dog for their bitch in haphazard fashion – either by pure fancy and guesswork or merely because the dog is fashionable. A sire to be of use to you should conform to the following essentials:

(a) Has proved himself as a good and regular stock-getter of high quality Cockers.
(b) Is himself well-bred and eminently suited to the breeding of your bitch.
(c) Can claim good-looks, masculinity and be absolutely sound in all departments as well as in rude health.

The big and famous winner, he who comes close to the long-sought-after 'perfect specimen' is not one iota of use to you unless he qualifies in the above points. If he is too young and not had time to prove his worth as a quality stock-getter, then let someone else be the guinea pig and try him out. Using any unknown quantity can do your breeding plan a deal of harm, even setting it back several generations. Do not worry if the dog you choose for your bitch is a bit big, even a shade coarse, so long as he is sound, healthy and teeming with great Cocker type and character. It is generally accepted that dogs sire their best stock when mature – youngsters on being tried out for the first time can produce nice puppies, but these seem often to lack the strength, vigour and substance of their later litters. Likewise puppies born to old parents often come from small litters, lacking good dentition and constitution. This does not necessarily apply to a stud dog who has been able to show and prove his pre-potency up to a late age. He would have been in regular use all his life and able to pass on his good qualities almost up to his death. Such a stud is a highly valued possession and seldom fails to make for himself a strong mark in the breed.

The bitch in season

The average bitch has her first season (or heat, as it is sometimes known) when she is nine months old, then every six months thereafter. The age for her first heat, also the frequency of the succeeding seasons may vary according to the individual, but this need occasion no alarm unless some abnormality is obvious. A heat lasts about three weeks, the first indication of an impending heat being an enlargement or swelling of the region abounding the vagina, with a mucous discharge which continues for a few days. This is followed by a show of 'colour' or blood and the day this is noted can be stated the first day of season. The bloodstained discharge will continue steadily for about a week and can be heavy, but by the ninth or tenth day it begins to wane until around the twelfth day it is either slight or has disappeared entirely. By this day, the bitch is usually ready for mating and she can be introduced to the dog who is to serve her. Although she may be 'ripe' for mating and this is shown usually by the stud dog's attitude towards her, if she is a maiden bitch it is likely that she will prove coy and coquettish. This is why many breeders prefer to arrange for an experienced stud dog to attend to maidens – the mating is then more expeditious, for the good dog tolerates no shyness. It can sometimes be ascertained when a bitch is ready for a dog's attentions by the way she tenses herself and holds her tail to one side when a hand is placed just on the croup. However, it is unlikely that any mating can be achieved without her full co-operation. Bitches vary considerably; some being quite ready to be served on the conventional twelfth day of their heat, others evincing a preference for a union on the ninth or even the fifteenth day of their heat. Generally speaking, it is better to contrive a bitch's mating at least before the fourteenth day or she may go over her time of ripeness and have to be held over from breeding for another six months. Once her idiosyncrasies are known however, she can be introduced to the dog at the time which suits her and no problems will exist.

The season lasts three weeks and she should be safeguarded the whole of this time, whether mated or not. Should she escape and be mated by a mongrel soon after her 'official' union, it is likely that his puppies will take precedence over the pure-bred ones, although your veterinary surgeon can with an injection ensure that she does not conceive. Unfortunately, puppies born of a misalliance, especially when the unwanted suitor looks like a Spaniel can appear true Spaniels even up to two months of age. Later when they reveal their impurity it is essential to ensure that they are not bred from.

There are a number of excellent preparations available for safe-guarding a bitch in season from the attentions of unwanted suitors. These range from aromatic oils to be applied externally to deodorants which must be given orally. These are generally quite effective, although it is not unknown for a really keen stud to remain undeterred in spite of them.

Most bitches in season keep themselves clean, but with some the flow is so excessive in the first week of heat that it will become necessary either to confine them to a spare room or kennel or to employ one of the sanitary belts for dogs which are now sold.

GESTATION CHART
This Table gives date of mating with expected date of whelping, based on the conventional 63-day period.

TABLE SHOWING WHEN A BITCH IS DUE TO WHELP

Served Jan. Whelps March	Served Feb. Whelps April	Served March Whelps May	Served April Whelps June	Served May Whelps July	Served June Whelps Aug.	Served July Whelps Sept.	Served Aug. Whelps Oct.	Served Sept. Whelps Nov.	Served Oct. Whelps Dec.	Served Nov. Whelps Jan.	Served Dec. Whelps Feb.
1 5	1 5	1 3	1 3	1 3	1 3	1 2	1 3	1 3	1 3	1 3	1 2
2 6	2 6	2 4	2 4	2 4	2 4	2 3	2 4	2 4	2 4	2 4	2 3
3 7	3 7	3 5	3 5	3 5	3 5	3 4	3 5	3 5	3 5	3 5	3 4
4 8	4 8	4 6	4 6	4 6	4 6	4 5	4 6	4 6	4 6	4 6	4 5
5 9	5 9	5 7	5 7	5 7	5 7	5 6	5 7	5 7	5 7	5 7	5 6
6 10	6 10	6 8	6 8	6 8	6 8	6 7	6 8	6 8	6 8	6 8	6 7
7 11	7 11	7 9	7 9	7 9	7 9	7 8	7 9	7 9	7 9	7 9	7 8
8 12	8 12	8 10	8 10	8 10	8 10	8 9	8 10	8 10	8 10	8 10	8 9
9 13	9 13	9 11	9 11	9 11	9 11	9 10	9 11	9 11	9 11	9 11	9 10
10 14	10 14	10 12	10 12	10 12	10 12	10 11	10 12	10 12	10 12	10 12	10 11
11 15	12 15	11 13	11 13	11 13	11 13	11 12	11 13	11 13	11 13	11 13	11 12
12 16	13 16	12 14	12 14	12 14	12 14	12 13	12 14	12 14	12 14	12 14	12 13
13 17	14 17	13 15	13 15	13 15	13 15	13 14	13 15	13 15	13 15	13 15	13 14
14 18	15 18	14 16	14 16	14 16	14 16	14 15	14 16	14 16	14 16	14 16	14 15
15 19	16 19	15 17	15 17	15 17	15 17	15 16	15 17	15 17	15 17	15 17	15 16
16 20	17 20	16 18	16 18	16 18	16 18	16 17	16 18	16 18	16 18	16 18	16 17
17 21	18 21	17 19	17 19	17 19	17 19	17 18	17 19	17 19	17 19	17 19	17 18
18 22	19 22	18 20	18 20	18 20	18 20	18 19	18 20	18 20	18 20	18 20	18 19
19 23	20 23	19 21	19 21	19 21	19 21	19 20	19 21	19 21	19 21	19 21	19 20
20 24	21 24	20 22	20 22	20 22	20 22	20 21	20 22	20 22	20 22	20 22	20 21
21 25	22 25	21 23	21 23	21 23	21 23	21 22	21 23	21 23	21 23	21 23	21 22
22 26	23 26	22 24	22 24	22 24	22 24	22 23	22 24	22 24	22 24	22 24	22 23
23 27	24 27	23 25	23 25	23 25	23 25	23 24	23 25	23 25	23 25	23 25	23 24
24 28	25 28	24 26	24 26	24 26	24 26	24 25	24 26	24 26	24 26	24 26	24 25
25 29	26 29	25 27	25 27	25 27	25 27	25 26	25 27	25 27	25 27	25 27	25 26
26 30	27 30	26 28	26 28	26 28	26 28	26 27	26 28	26 28	26 28	26 28	26 27
27 31	28 1	27 29	27 29	27 29	27 29	27 28	27 29	27 29	27 29	27 29	27 28
28 1	29 2	28 30	28 30	28 30	28 30	28 29	28 30	28 30	28 30	28 30	28 1
29 2		29 31	29 1	29 31	29 31	29 30	29 31	29 1	29 31	29 31	29 2
30 3		30 1	30 2	30 1	30 1	30 1	30 1	30 2	30 1	30 1	30 3
31 4		31 2		31 2		31 2	31 2		31 2		31 4

Mating

Many people ask which is the best day for mating their bitch to the dog. The simplest answer to this is the *right* day and this can vary from bitch to bitch. It is true that matings can often be arranged satisfactorily during the latter part of the bitch's second week of season, i.e. about the twelfth day from when she commenced to show 'colour'. The really successful mating will occur on the day when she is discharging here ova to be fertilised by the dog's sperms, her red flow by this time dispersing, even having disappeared. She will show her readiness for the dog by standing with her hindquarters tensed and with the tail held to one side. She will do this even when the dog is not present and it is then time to introduce her to the dog. He will take stock of the situation and with some preliminary courtship will mount her and thrust with his penis at her vulva.

It should be said at this point that until both animals have proved their friendliness to each other, initial introductions should be with both of them on collar and lead. If the bitch is experienced and the dog is not, she will stand steady and help to expedite his entry. In fact, it is always a good idea to let a young dog have his initial mating with a matron in order to educate him for future affairs. The same applies when a maiden bitch is being mated; she being better with an old-stager who will encourage her with his mating skill to co-operate with minimal fuss. The main thing is to get the mating over and done with while preserving the natural methods of effecting it. Some mating pairs will proceed with the job at once, performing a natural mating without any manual aid from the handlers.

However, it is not unusual to have just a little trouble, especially when one of the dogs is not used to the proceedings. The bitch may become coquettish and snap round at her suitor, or roll on her back in a ridiculous fashion! The dog, if a sheer novice, may in his excitement start to mount the wrong end! Such clowning is well-known in breeding circles and if a bitch acts this way she will need to be stood up and supported. If she continues to bite she may have to be tape-muzzled, but this should be done only as a last resort. She should be wearing a strap collar (so should the dog) and her owner should clasp this, the heel of each hand on either side of her face, steadying her from making a sudden turn round, at the time talking to her reassuringly. The stud dog's owner should be at the rear end, one hand under the bitch's loins propping up her hindquarters thereby taking part of the dog's weight as he mounts and begins to thrust. He may need to guide the dog into her, but if the stud seems to be making entry unaided, he should be left to it. Once he has entered he will thrust in deep; the bitch if she is a maiden may cry out at this, but the pain will be only momentary and she will soon stand firm again. When the dog makes entry it will help if his owner presses him in just above his tail, holding him tight against the bitch's body for fifteen seconds or so. This will facilitate the making of a tie, which is usually considered conclusive proof of a satisfactory mating, with every chance of fruition. The tie is made by a bulb or circular gland of tissue which swells out from the shaft of the dog's penis and becomes gripped by a ring of muscle at the mouth of the bitch's vulva. Once this hold has been established the mating pair should be brought round tail-to-tail. Some dogs achieve the position naturally, but take time doing it. They can be helped by easing round the dog, dropping one foreleg across and over the bitch's body so that both forelegs are on the same side. At the same time, gently raise one hind-leg from the 'off-side' and bring that too over and across the bitch's back, swivelling round the dog's body meanwhile until the pair are standing rump to rump. This is the natural mating position of dogs in the wild. It provides for a mating armament to be at both ends of the diameter of a turning circle. Thus, if the occupied two are attacked while still tied they can turn in any direction and protect themselves.

The tie lasts between twenty and thirty minutes as a rule and during this time the pair will be fairly at ease, copulation proceeding meanwhile. The owners should not relax their observation however, and when it becomes apparent that they will disengage, the dog should be slipped on his lead and the bitch transferred at once to her kennel for a rest. Later, she can be fed and watered. The dog should have his comfort attended to, making sure that the sheath has returned properly over his penis. He too can now be watered and fed.

It is seldom that more than one service will be required in such circumstances, but when a young and a possibly unproven dog has been used it is best to let him serve the bitch again within thirty-six hours. Quite apart from the practice it gives him, it is believed that the first service will act as a stimulant to the second, and this may be true.

Pre-natal care of the bitch

The usual period between conception and birth is sixty-three days, although a bitch having her first litter may not conform to the rules, having her puppies a day or so earlier or later. There is no hard and fast rule about this, but sixty-three days is a reasonable average to plan with and a gestation chart or breeding table will be found on page 51. There is not a lot to do with an in-whelp bitch except to step up the nutritive feeding and ensure she is not put into a situation where she could be involved in an accident. Her health and fitness at this time is very important. She should have been thoroughly de-wormed just prior to mating and some breeders repeat the dosage about two weeks after the mating date.

She should be well-fed with an emphasis on fresh raw meat and proteins. Her exercise should be maintained as normal but not increased. At around the fifth or sixth week it should be apparent that she is in whelp by the thickening in the area of her loins. Cut down all starchy and farinaceous foods, biscuits and sweets being of little use to a bitch in whelp. Fish is particularly good and herrings, if in season, will do her good. As she gets near to her time reduce her exercise proportionately, but make sure she gets her daily walk, however brief, right up to the time she is expected to produce her puppies. About ten days before the happy event she can be given a teaspoonful of medicinal paraffin with her evening meal. This will oil her up nicely inside and should make the whelping a little easier. At least ten days before she is due, she should be introduced to prepared whelping quarters. This can be a quietly situated garden shed arranged as a whelping kennel and made free from draughts, or a spare room on ground level. A proper whelping box should be installed and one can be constructed by any handyman. It should be about 24 in. by 30 in., bounded on three sides by walls which stand about 18 in. high. The remaining side should be hinged so that it can be let down like a drawbridge to control the comings and goings of the puppies, once they get old enough. Provide a 'pig rail' all round the sides of the whelping box – this being 1 in. by 2 in. wood set in about 3 in. to 4 in. above floor level. The tiny whelps can shelter under the projection this affords from a clumsy dam, liable to jump into the nest or to flop down without warning on to her young.

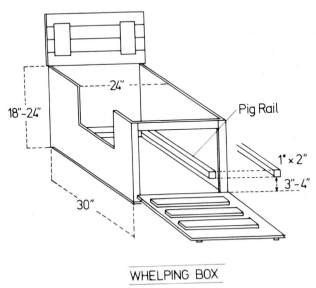

WHELPING BOX

FIG. 3. WHELPING BOX

It is advisable to raise all beds away from draughts. Only an inch above floor level will serve its purpose and protect dam and litter. Try and arrange for the mother to have a bed of her own well out of the way of her puppies. She will appreciate this, especially when the puppies become demanding in later weeks. An infra-red lamp is a useful accessory, and worth its cost. It should be fitted to the ceiling and can be raised or lowered at will to control the temperature required. Providing the lamp is well protected and made safe from falling it will help the newborn puppies to thrive and will more than pay for its initial outlay.

Whelping

If a bitch seems to be going beyond her normal whelping time of sixty-three days it is advisable to call in your veterinary surgeon, especially if she seems to be getting distressed at the delay. He may inject her to hasten delivery, but this should be done only if absolutely necessary. The same rule applies to a Caesarian section which a long overdue bitch may require to save not only her own life but those of her puppies.

The first sign given by a bitch about to whelp is refusal of food and restless behaviour. Her normal temperature should be 101.4° and if this drops more than 2° and/or she seems very upset, then call your veterinary surgeon. At this stage the bitch should be in her prepared bed. A bitch left to her own devices is liable to find the most inconvenient (as far as her owner is concerned) quarters for her young. Line the bottom of the whelping box or pen with clean hessian or newspapers so that she has something to tear and scratch up in labour. This is much better than straw or blankets which puppies can get underneath and be smothered.

A tacky discharge will appear at the mouth of the vagina when she is ready to whelp and her temperature will drop about 2°+ from normal. Soon she will fall into a deep sleep which will relax her and prepare her for the rigorous time ahead of her. When she is ready to deliver her first puppy she will begin to pant and some rippling of the muscles across the back will be noted. Matters can usually be hastened by giving her a drink of warm milk, but this need not be done as it is better to let things take an uninterrupted course. Contractions will increase as the first puppy draws near until there are three or four strains in about the same number of minutes. Eventually, the water bag – a small water-filled balloon about the size of a golf ball will appear at the mouth of the vulva. This acts as a cushion protecting the oncoming puppy. It will break or be broken by the bitch herself, the puppy following almost at once. Should there be any untoward delay and two hours pass without sight of the whelp, the veterinary surgeon had better be called in to deal with the problem. However, if all goes well, the puppy should arrive head first this being a normal delivery. Sometimes it will arrive feet first, this being known as a breech birth and one seldom if every presenting a complication, certainly not in Cockers. It is when a puppy is presented sideways or is lodged in an unnatural position in the passage that a dangerous situation can arise, necessitating immediate veterinary action.

The puppy will arrive in a membranous sac, rather like a polythene bag. This bag may be broken in the course of the birth, but if not the bitch will break it so that the puppy can gulp in air and begin to breathe. Should the dam fail in her instinctive reaction or have an undershot jaw which might make it difficult for her to nip through the sac, the job must be done for her. The breeder should quickly insert a finger at the end where the puppy's head lies, exposing it to the air. The bitch should then lick the whelp vigorously and buffet it with her tongue to induce respiration. The puppy will still be attached by the umbilical cord to the afterbirth or placenta which will still be inside the dam. By holding the cord at the puppy's end, making sure that no pull is made away from the puppy itself the placenta can sometimes be drawn out.

It need not surprise you if the bitch promptly eats it for this is nature's way of giving a whelping mother sustenance and it does no harm. However, some breeders prefer to dispose of it and feed the bitch with warm milk to which a little glucose has been added. It should be noted that for every puppy there is a placenta and it is important to count the puppies in relation to the placentae when the bitch has finished whelping. This will ensure that no afterbirth remains in her which might cause a septic womb condition later.

Another of the bitch's tasks is to nip through the umbilical cord near to the puppy's navel; again if she fails to do it, it must be done for her. Take a pair of sterilised scissors and cut the cord about half-an-inch to an inch from the little one's navel, tying it tightly with a short length of surgical cord near to the body. Take care not to pull the cord away from the puppy's body or an unsightly umbilical hernia may be formed. The puppies will be born at frequent intervals, probably every fifteen or twenty minutes, the intervals extending in length as the later ones arrive. So long as there is no really serious delay this need cause no alarm. The puppies after being cleaned by their dam will begin to suckle at her immediately and once she is seen cleaning herself and acting calmly it is probable that she has finished her ordeal. This is the time to try and get her outside, not only to relieve herself, but to check on her puppies for their sex and the presence of any abnormalities. The whelping box should also be cleaned up too while she is away, the sacking or newspapers being disposed of and fresh bedding introduced. She is then best left with her family in a quiet dark room, no strangers being allowed to intrude for several days.

The prudent breeder may prefer to equip himself with a first-aid kit comprising all the things he is likely to need should he be called upon to help in whelping. A recommended outfit would be as follows:

1. A pair of good quality, sharp, sterilised probe pointed surgical scissors.
2. A new packet of large paper tissues, also a few squares of surgical lint or muslin pieces about nine inches square, for grasping the whelps.
3. Several cut lengths of surgical thread about six inches long.
4. A bottle of prepared disinfectant solution about 1:5, and a stronger disinfectant for swabbing down. Some 'Vaseline'.
5. Rubber gloves, sterilised and laid out on a dry, clean towel.
6. Several pieces of dry, clean white turkish terry towelling.
7. Stone hot-water bottle, suitably covered for potection.
8. A feeding bottle, also a bowl.
9. Brandy to be given (only if required) a drop or two at a time from a teaspoon.
10. A kettle ready filled with water, standing-by.

POST-NATAL MATTERS

The ideal litter is five or six puppies, a number like this obtaining maximum benefit from the natural feeding of an average bitch. Unwieldly litters are inclined to wear down the dam after a few weeks and unless she is reinforced substantially with extra nutritive feeding she is liable to debilitate. This would be not only to her disadvantage but to her puppies who would receive a set-back in their development.

It is possible that some of the puppies, reverting to an early ancestor will be mismarked, this in spite of your careful planning. The decision then has to be made as to whether you will dispose these humanely (which is really better for the breed in general) or run them on and find them homes as pets. A decision such as this is probably easier made when a litter is too big and likely to prove embarrassing for the dam to feed later on. On the other hand, if the litter is a big one and of good quality it might be wise to bring in a foster mother (see relevant section). If this is done it must be arranged at once, the mother and foster mother being kept at a discreet distance from each other.

The bitch, for some days after whelping will pass very loose motions, the afterbirths she will have eaten causing these to be dark and pungent. No alarm need be felt, for this is normal; nevertheless you should make an effort to clear up the condition and your veterinary surgeon will prescribe a suitable preparation. The bitch should now be feeding her puppies and generally enjoying their attentions. Her feeding (as recommended in the chapter on this subject) should be well balanced, highly nutritive and with plenty of protein. The milk flow should be ample and care taken that the whelps are all getting their fair share. Sometimes the greedy members of a litter will attempt to 'hog' the lot by attaching themselves to the most rewarding teats (the inguinal) situated in the groin. Watch for such greediness and ensure that the less pushing puppies take their fair turn where the most milk flows.

The dam should be having plenty of milk to drink and fresh cool water should be readily available to her. This will aid her milk supply for water and raw meat are the best milk producers.

Bitches do not like being removed too far from their family within the first week of motherhood, so exercise will have to be contrived discreetly at first, it being very necessary to keep her healthy and build up her milk supply.

Dew-claws and docking

Dew-claws are the rudimentary fifth digit on the forelegs (and sometimes on the hind legs) equivalent to the thumb in humans and likely to prove a nuisance to a dog if allowed to remain. Most breeders remove them when the puppies are four days old, providing the whelps were not prematurely born when this minor operation should be left for a few days longer. This will ensure they receive no set-back. Using a pair of snub-nosed surgical scissors which have been properly sterilised, these little appendages can be removed with a deft cut, the wounds being dabbed with Friars' Balsam, crushed permanganate of potash crystals or similar styptic. Few puppies appear to actually feel the operation but in case one should cry out it is kind to keep the dam well out of earshot until it is all over to avoid upsetting her.

Tail docking can be done at the same time as the dew-claws, although some breeders prefer to do it about thirty-six hours later. Again, if the puppies are in good health it is best to get such operations over and done with. Similar scissors as employed for the dew-claws should be used, the specific requirements for a Cocker being to leave on about one-third of the tail. The usual point for cutting is where the thick part of the cartilage joins the thin part. This should be easily ascertained and the cut made cleanly and confidently *after* the tail skin has been drawn back towards the set-on. Then when the cut has been made the released skin will elasticate back just slightly beyond the wound stump, protecting it and aiding the healing. The wounds should be sterilised as for dew-claws and examined several times daily to ensure they are clean and healthy.

The above operations should not be attempted by an amateur who has never before seen them done professionally or by a person who is nervous. Quite apart from being unfair to the animals concerned, a good litter of Cockers can be ruined with haphazard docking, and when too much tail is removed it can never be rectified. When a veterinary surgeon is engaged to dock your puppies' tails, make quite sure that he is fully conversant with the breed's requirements as to finished length of tail. Fortunately, the Cocker being a popular variety most vets know what is wanted but it is worth checking to save an embarrassing situation later.

Fading puppies

This is an unfortunate condition often affecting an entire litter, sometimes just two or three of its members. Although it is fairly common, little appears to be known as to its cause. Some veterinary experts have blamed a dam's poor health and constitution, others claim the cause lies with bad conditions of housing and management at whelping time. The usual symptoms are that whereas a litter is born apparently lusty and well, some or all of them gradually get weak and unhappy, finally dying off without apparent cause. The deterioration process may take anything from a few hours after birth to several days.

When fading is suspected, veterinary advice should be sought at once. Certain injections have proved helpful and penicillin has been used with success when infection is suspected to contribute to the condition, both the dam and her puppies being treated. The aftermath of Canine Virus Hepatitis, its effects being passed from the dam to her brood has been given as a responsible factor in fading but this may be just one of several likely reasons for the tragic loss of litters which is becoming too common for comfort. It emphasises the need for ensuring that both parents are in good health at mating time and quite free from worms. That the whelping procedure is disciplined and well managed becomes important too – every effort being made to ensure that the bitch's instinctive whelping functions at this time are not subjected to unnecessary interference by human agency. Her food too should be fresh and wholesome; her exercise planned to improve her mental awareness as well as her body.

Nursing problems

Even in the best planned breeding programme, things sometimes go wrong and it is as well to be prepared for such eventualities. A common occurrence is lack of milk at a vital time, i.e. when the puppies are first born and need to avail themselves of the Colostrum which is present in the initial flow. This substance contains a valuable immunising agent which protects the whelps from disease during the first few weeks of their lives. The condition of Aglactia or lack of milk, seldom lasts longer than a few days, but it must be dealt with immediately. If prompt veterinary action to counteract this hormone deficiency proves fruitless then the breeder has two courses open to him. One is to engage at once a foster parent and transfer his valuable puppies to her or to take on the thankless task of hand-rearing them from a pipette, using the recommended mixture of 'Lactol' or a similar substitute for bitch's milk. However, first he must arrange with his veterinary surgeon for the puppies to be injected with Gamahtine (gamma globulin) to recompense for the absent Colostrum. It is seldom that a bitch will remain without milk for more than a few days, total Aglactia being rare. The puppies will always thrive best on their dam's milk and every effort should be made to induce a reasonable flow so that they can be settled down as a normal happy family. This can be achieved by continually putting the puppies on to her teats and by gently kneading and massaging the breasts in the hope that milk will flow. The bitch should be encouraged to drink plenty of fluids which should help. Providing her inability to feed her young does not appear to disturb the bitch, the puppies meanwhile being hand-reared are best maintained by her side, thus keeping them warm naturally and ensuring that they are under her watchful eye. Keep the bitch well fed on fresh raw meat and see that she drinks as much cold water as possible. This type of intake will encourage the flow of milk and coupled with plenty of daily exercise the dam should soon be able to take over her brood, proceeding normally and contentedly.

Another disturbing condition liable to affect the bitch is the reverse of Aglactia; it is excess of milk. It can occur with a hearty dam whose litter is small, perhaps only one or two puppies; or whose main brood has died at time of whelping. In such cases her fluid intake should be drastically reduced and the breeder should endeavour to express some of the surplus milk from her. The way to achieve this is to stand her on her hind legs and manually exert the teats which will spurt off some of the milk. There is a danger that this will encourage even more milk to develop, but as the puppies grow on and require more sustenance this will not matter. The main thing is to ease her discomfort in the very early stages. If the situation gets desperate and she seems to be filled with milk, the teats being hard, swollen and sore, then your veterinary surgeon will be able to inject her to disperse it, but discretion must be used while there remains even one puppy requiring food.

There are other problems a breeder might have to contend with apart from the foregoing, a disturbing one being the bitch who kills her puppies one by one as they are born. Fortunately, such a bad mother is rare and should not be bred from thereafter. If it seems certain such a dam might destroy all the litter, the only way to cope with the matter is to take each puppy as soon as it is born and segregate it immediately, making sure that it is warm and safe from its mother. Collect the remainder in this way, hand feed until a foster parent becomes available and deal with the bitch as for excess of milk.

The Caesarian operation

The secret of making a successful Caesarian section is based largely on its careful timing. A qualified and experienced veterinary surgeon will be able to determine this, but the owner too should be sufficiently well acquainted with the behaviour pattern of his bitch in whelp (assuming she is not having puppies for the first time) as to help in the decision.

Although the operation is quite an easy one from a veterinary viewpoint it should never be attempted unless absolutely necessary, as it is fraught with hazards for the breeder who might lose both bitch and her unborn young if something went wrong. A major risk is that the latter are frequently anaesthetised when their mother is rendered unconscious and become very difficult to revive when born, consequently many are lost when born from a Caesarian section. Some veterinary surgeons use a form of anaesthetic which while putting the bitch into a deep sleep has no effect on her young, thereby reducing the mortality rate considerably.

The usual time to start a Caesarian operation, all conditions being satisfactory, is just before the bitch has become exhausted due to protracted and unsuccessful labour, certainly ere she has lapsed into a panic because of the hold-up. The science of the operation is today so well understood that she is unlikely to suffer any after-effects from it, most patients being calm and normal and enjoying the attentions of their puppies an hour or so after regaining consciousness. At this stage it is important to leave the family well alone, preferably in a warm room away from strangers and would-be admirers. Some breeders use stone hot water bottles in the pen, but these should be covered with blankets for the protection of the bitch and whelps.

Hand rearing

This is not really a task for even the most dedicated breeder to relish. It requires unlimited patience, a good deal of affection for one's stock as well as many hours loss of sleep, for small puppies require feeding at regular intervals during the night just as they do during the daylight hours. However, if a bitch has died in whelp and her puppies are orphaned or she is sick and unable to cope with them, they must be tended.

The busiest time in hand rearing is usually during the first fortnight, although it could extend into the third week of the youngsters' lives if they are slow to thrive. The important factors involved in hand rearing are not only a maintained regular temperature but frequent well balanced feeds and scrupulous hygiene. There are some excellent fortified milk foods on the market specially designed for bottle feeding and directions for their use will be found with these preparations. The instructions should be followed faithfully, especially with regard to the temperature at which they should be fed and the amount given at each meal.

4-week old puppies

The 'nest' where the puppies are kept should be heated to a steady and cosy temperature. This can be achieved by placing one, even two hot water bottles (stone ones are best) under or around the bed, making sure they do not make actual contact with the whelps. It will be found wiser to under-feed than to give too much for it is easy to upset such a small puppy's digestion and once disturbed its effect can remain with a dog all his life. Feeding should take place every two hours day and night for the first ten days, then relapse into three-hourly intervals for the next week, using a baby's feeding bottle. The food should be at about 100°F., a consistency about three times the strength of cow's milk being ideal. Some people incorporate a drop of lime juice into the daily ration to help digestion, others like to dose each puppy with a single drop of halibut liver oil every twenty-four hours. It is important to maintain the same heat of feeding for each puppy. This can be done by keeping the cup of milk mixture in a bowl of hot water and keeping it stirred. The feeding bottle should be wrapped round with a heat-retaining cloth and shaken at intervals to distribute the mixture properly.

If the dam was looking after her puppies she would stimulate their urination and motions by licking their parts, the wetness and warmth of her tongue having its immediate effect. With a piece of cotton wool which has been dampened in warm water the breeder must wipe round the private parts and anal regions of every puppy. This will cause both water and motions to be passed, and this is essential before or after each meal for any blockage in a small puppy's intestines is likely to be fatal. The parts should then be smeared with a little grease such as 'Vaseline' and the youngster's mouth and nostrils wiped around to dispose of any congealed milk which might adhere.

When the puppies are three weeks old normal weaning can commence, finely shredded raw meat being introduced to the diet, by which time the meals can be staggered a little. This means that night feeding can be brought down to only three meals between midnight and 8 a.m. but during the day meals should be maintained every three hours.

It will be realised that hand-reared puppies are seldom as forward as those which have been naturally raised, which means that feeding during weaning needs to be on a fairly high grade to compensate for any acquired deficiencies. By the time the puppies are five weeks old they should be on three meat and two milk meals daily, care being taken that they are not over-fed at any meal.

THE INFRA-RED LAMP

The regular breeder of Cocker Spaniels should invest in a reliable infra-red lamp. This is not only an efficient accessory when rearing puppies generally, but when it becomes important to maintain a steady temperature such as required by hand-reared puppies, such a lamp becomes almost an essential.

A lamp fitted with a dull-emitter bulb is preferable, for it cannot irritate the bitch's eyes, but make sure that the reflector is adequately protected with a wire guard to prevent any part of it becoming loose and falling on the family below. Secure the whole unit firmly at a safe height above the bed or bench with a thermometer easily accessible and visible yet out of the dam's way. The ideal temperature to maintain in the case of a newly born litter is 75°. This can be reduced by 5° by the end of the first week by raising the lamp level very slightly every day, checking the thermometer hourly to control the heat in relation to outside warmth. The kennel heat can be reduced a further 5° in the following week and so on until the lamp's effect is no longer needed.

The lamp can be used at any time an invalid dog needs nursing after sickness or surgery. Always take the temperature from bed level alongside the dog so as to ascertain the degree of heat actually reaching the animal. The usual wattage of these lamps is 200 or 250, but most canine requisite suppliers can supply from a fairly wide range of types and qualities to suit the breeders specific needs.

The foster mother

If your bitch has a bad record as a mother, it is advisable to arrange for a foster mother to be standing by at the expected date of whelping. Some people prefer to have the bitch in their home a few days earlier in order to give her time to settle down and become used to her new surroundings with its fresh smells and new faces. Certainly, this is better than waiting twenty-four hours or more for her to arrive following your emergency call. Some kennels specialise in the supply of such foster parents, maintaining such breeds as Collies and Setters, noted for their prolific milk supply when nursing. On receiving your S.O.S. the kennel would dispose one of its inmate's puppies and rail the dam to you immediately. On arrival, apart from the foster's natural distraction at losing her puppies and being sent away, she would normally accept your waiting puppies without objection. They in turn would at once suckle at her and all would soon settle down contentedly, although it is best to introduce her new family to her one by one, just in case of accident!

Before importing a foster dam, first have her vetted in her own locality by a qualified veterinary surgeon, who for a nominal fee will determine her good health or otherwise and ensure that she is free from lice, etc. Such a wise precaution could save you the disaster and expense of a lost litter due to an infection brought in by a diseased bitch. However, most foster dam service kennels, especially the regular advertisers in the weekly dog journals have a good name for clean stock and reliability.

False pregnancies

This condition appears to have increased within the last decade. The bitch, following the usual period of gestation, exhibits all the usual signs of being in whelp and acts just as though she expects a litter, starting to make up a 'nest' and showing all the temperamental signs of an animal expecting a happy event. Such indications may occur even when the bitch has never had a dog near her at mating time, her symptoms being exactly as one genuinely and correctly mated. Naturally, the owner who is fully aware of his bitch's detachment from any sire will more readily recognise the fact that his charge is in a state of false pregnancy, but when a litter has been planned and eagerly anticipated the situation can be fraught with worry and disappointment. In some instances the bitch will carry inanimate objects to her whelping box or bed and become generally quite distressed with the whole affair. The udders will often fill with milk, ready to feed her imaginary puppies and at such times it may be necessary to sedate her, so bemused and upset may she become. It is important to keep close to her and offer reassurance for at least a week following the inevitable disappointment, and the veterinary surgeon should examine her and will probably inject and prescribe oral hormones. It is not unusual for such bitches to make a habit of these false alarms and the owner should be forewarned that he may have a bitch on his hands unlikely to be of much good as a breeder or even to be quite barren. However, it may be that with care and persistence, the bitch could be brought round to motherhood as the veterinary field has plenty of suggestions which could be adopted. Clearly, the cause is connected either with lack of certain hormones or some chemical imbalance; hereditary conditions do not appear to be totally responsible. With persistent repetition of the condition the only infallible cure would seem to be an ovario-hysterectomy as a last resort.

4 Feeding

Weaning and small puppy feeding

Most Cocker puppies are ready for the important process of weaning by the time they are about 3½ weeks old. This assumes that both the dam and her litter are healthy and contented and the bitch's milk flow is rich and adequate; also that the brood is not more than six in number. Should the litter be large and unwieldy, say eight or more and the dam's milk supply seems over-taxed then better start weaning at 3 weeks to aid the building-up process and to ease the mother.

Remember, the dam's feeding is most important especially while she is lactating. It should be comprised of liberal meals of fresh, raw, juicy meat, eggs, steamed white fish (which has been carefully boned) and plenty of liquids, especially milk. You may find when the puppies are ready for weaning their mother will regurgitate some of her own partly-digested food. This need occasion no alarm; some owners fear a stomach upset when they see this occur for the first time, but it is merely her way of aiding the weaning of her young. Nevertheless, it is advisable when feeding the dam to cut or chop up her meat a good bit smaller than is usual with an adult, just in case she disgorges food which her puppies might choke on. Obviously, when a bitch throws up her meals in this manner, she is likely to go hungry unless she is re-fed. Not only this but without nutriment she will speedily weaken and be unable to maintain the efficient rearing of her litter. Because of this try and arrange her own feeding an hour or two prior to the puppies' weaning meals for this will allow time for her digestion to be reasonably complete and regurgitation more difficult.

The puppies must first be taught to lap. A good preparation which can be relied upon as near to bitch's milk is 'Lactol'. Many breeders use it and find it simple to make and administer. Full instructions as to mixing will be found on the canister and a heaped tablespoonful is usually enough for a small puppy, mixed to the consistency of thick cream in hot water and whipped to an emulsified finish. More hot water should then be added until it is like thin cream. It is now ready for feeding and should be at blood heat temperature. Maintain the temperature of the liquid by standing the bowl in a pan of hot water so that every puppy is fed at similar warmth.

To commence, stand a clean shallow feeding vessel on a clean dry towel and spoon in about four teaspoonsful of the mixture. Then take a puppy, place him down next to the bowl and gently press his head and nose down to the milky food. He will probably draw back as his nose touches it, but once he has sensed the 'Lactol' by its taste and warmth he should start to lap, following some initial spluttering. If he seems dubious, smear a little of the milk on your finger tip and insert it under the youngster's lips. The average puppy absorbs the food with relish and is quickly encouraged to lap freely henceforth. Once the entire litter is ready to move on to more solid provender, introduce them to light milk puddings, arrowroot, boiled fish, poached and scrambled egg dishes, then finely shredded fresh raw meat and minced raw tripe. The way they begin to thrive from this point will be marked and your main task then will be to ensure that the gluttonous ones take no advantage over the slower feeders by hogging the major part of the food. Watch too for the impetuous feeders who dive head first into the bowl, guarding against this by raising the dish an inch or two from the ground on a shallow box or similar. This idea has the added merit of encouraging a good 'head-up' posture, as well as protecting the ears, which should be maintained throughout the dog's life.

Ensure that the puppies and their quarters are kept scrupulously clean; this means apart from swabbing out and disinfecting their living quarters with regular precision, their personal comfort should be attended to. See they pass good motions, semi-firm or with the consistency of porridge. Make sure no faeces remain adhering to the anal regions and inspect every puppy twice a day for health and soundness. Watch to see that no undue distension occurs after eating; evidence of this may indicate over-eating or heavy worm infestation. There are a number of reliable proprietary brands of medicine to deal simply enough with the parasites which beset most puppies and instructions for their use can be found on the packet and followed with confidence. Today, worming can be attempted soon after weaning has commenced, but if you are in doubt as to a wise course of action consult your veterinary surgeon.

By the time the puppies are five weeks old and on foods of thicker consistency than milk they should be on three small meals a day increasing to four to five meals a day at six weeks, by which time the dam should either be free from them or at least not too much in evidence, for by now her puppies should be virtually independent of her. Their food can be increased now, fresh raw meat taking precedence over the other solids, but supported well with puppy meal such as 'Saval No. 1'. Milk should be available and this should have the chill taken off it, as cold milk – especially that straight from the refrigerator – is harmful to young stock. A suggested menu is as follows; the actual times of course can be adjusted to suit the owner:

7 a.m.   Milky meal, milk to have chill taken off. Mix with good name proprietary baby food, or wheat cereal or rusks. Porridge, etc.

11 a.m.   Meat meal, finely shredded (better than minced) fresh raw meat, some doggy biscuit meal soaked in stock or gravy. Strained vegetable juice added if available. Alternatively, steamed boned fish.

3 p.m.   Milky meal, similar to 7 a.m. meal.

7 p.m.   Meat meal, similar to 11 a.m. meal. Add teaspoonful of cod-liver oil.

11 p.m.   Saucer of warm milk.

In order to maintain the puppies at their peak it will be necessary to gauge their food intake so that you give neither too much nor too little. This applies especially to the meat meals. The average puppy is a voracious feeder; he has a good healthy appetite which approaches greediness. Watch them feed; they will fall into the meals without ado, but after an interval of eating will hesitate and take breath. This usually indicates the extent of their inner needs and from such a sign you should be able to assess how much food to put before each puppy. By acting on it you will avoid overfeeding them, always a dangerous thing to do with young stock.

By the time the puppy is about six months of age he can be on just two meals a day – a substantial and nourishing meat meal in the evening, preferably after exercising and a saucer of milk, possibly with rusks or dog biscuits at midday. As he matures, the quantity can be increased in proportion to his requirements, but the system of main meat meal in the evening with milk and biscuits for lunch can be maintained for the rest of his life, producing excellent results.

Feeding the adult dog

It is essential that your Cocker should be maintained in good bloom at all times, especially if you have aspirations for the show ring, when you will need to balance carefully those requirements which include feeding, exercising, training and grooming. A dog looks forward to his meal and if the food is fresh, good and enjoyable he thrives on it. Good food keeps him free from many everyday ailments which beset the poorly maintained dog and contributes much towards an insurance against veterinary costs. If you can afford fresh raw meat, give him this rather than believe the stories which tell you that paunches and offal sundries are better. The latter are only useful as stand-bys when fresh meat is unavailable, as are many commercial foods and fish. In fact, a dog should be got used to every kind of feeding and whereas raw meat is always preferable cut straight from the piece, you should try him out occasionally with cooked meat both cold and warm. In this way, you need never be nonplussed for a meal and he will be

ready and able to enjoy anything you have at hand in an emergency. A fastidious dog who will eat only one form of food is a nuisance and seldom thrives as well as a ready eater of mixed foods. Herrings when in season make excellent nutriment and these are best prepared in a pressure cooker. Try and feed dry whenever possible; he will benefit better from food served in this way. Regular mealtimes are important if you find it convenient, for the dog gets used to a certain time for his meal, best put down in the evening period by which time he will be ready to enjoy it and obtain advantage at the same time from its good effects. 'A fit dog is a happy dog' so the saying goes. It is a good motto for adoption by the conscientious Cocker owner.

Miss J. Macmillan and Mrs J. Gillespie's Norwegian and English Sh. Ch. Lochranza Man of Fashion

Vitamins

Vitamins are found in natural foods and in sunshine. No dog could exist in good health without an adequate supply and in the right amounts they will furnish him with all the basic nutrients he needs for goodness and contentment. Many ailments and diseases are believed to stem from a dog's feeding conditions and habits which are poorly endowed with the requisite vitamins. The conscientious Cocker owner should acquaint himself with some knowledge of the worth and effect of vitamins.

Vitamin A. Found in fish liver oils, heart and liver, eggs and milk. It is necessary for healthy skin tissue, bones and dentition. A valuable aid to keen eyesight it is used to counteract such conditions as 'night blindness', which is an inability to accept light after a period of darkness and vice versa. Parsley and raw carrots contain plenty of Vitamin A, which contributes to a dog's longevity.

Vitamin B. Referred to as B-Complex and found in wheat-germ, liver, yeast, milk, meat and eggs. It is good for the skin, nerves, appetite and coat. It aids growth and improves the blood.

Vitamin C. Obtained from grass which has absorbed it from the sun. It is invaluable as a general tonic, good for skin, dentition and growth. Milk is well stored with this vitamin.

Vitamin D. This builds bone and teeth with the use of calcium and phosphorus. It can be found in fish oils, eggs and liver oils. It is useful in breeding, being a safeguard against rickets and encouraging digestion.

Vitamin E. Wheat germ oil is the main source of this vitamin. It is a useful aid to fertility, therefore good for the active stud dog and an ideal insurance against dead puppies and absorbed foetuses in the brood bitch.

Most of the above vitamins can be taken by a dog through normal feeding of fresh raw meat, milk and eggs, coupled with plenty of sunshine, fresh air and an opportunity to tread and eat grass. However, the various vitamins are usually available in capsule form from pet stores and chemists catering for veterinary products.

5 Training

Early lessons

No one should buy a dog unless he is prepared to make a genuine effort, entailing time and considerable patience to train him properly. An ill-trained dog is a menace, not only to his owner and his friends, but to himself. On the other hand, a well-trained one is a much happier creature for he has learned to please his master as well as making his own lot a contented one. The master too becomes proud of his aptitude as a trainer and in effect, the two live happier together.

Elementary training can be commenced almost from the moment the puppy becomes yours and enters your home. The average youngster is usually quite willing to learn anything, but he has to be shown *how* to learn. This means you need to study the pupil's natural characteristics. Some puppies show a leaning towards training from the start, indicating quite plainly that they are conscious and thinking of all that goes on around them. Others seem to prefer more the pleasures of life, which although natural enough makes them more difficult to train. The first word to train a dog to understand is the word 'No'. This word lends itself well to authoritative command, being a word of brisk intonation. A lot of people incorporate with its use the administration of a rolled-up newspaper, which when applied to a disobedient puppy makes a whack but does not hurt, merely startling him into obedience. You can please yourself whether or not you utilise a newspaper, most puppies will react sufficiently to the spoken word – more stubborn characters may well need a more positive form of direction. As the owner becomes used to his dog and understands him better the other monosyllabic commands of 'Wait', 'Sit', 'Stay', 'Lie', 'Up' and 'Down' with their self-evident responses become quite easily involved in the dog's training.

HOUSE TRAINING

This is an important aspect of elementary training, especially of the pet dog. No owner should mind a puppy making the odd puddle or two during the first few weeks at home, but as the youngster grows and the puddles become proportionately larger, the constant attendance and cleaning up begins to pall. House-training should begin from the first day of ownership, but remember small puppies are just like babies – they cannot control their bowels and bladders. Again, like babies they spend most of their early days resting and sleeping and on waking they want to urinate. This instinctive sequence should be taken advantage of – it is no use waiting for a puppy to uncurl, stretch, climb out of bed, wander round the floor, then urinate – probably in an inaccessible corner of the kitchen! You must pick him up as soon as he opens his eyes, carry him to the garden door and deposit him outside, saying at the same time 'Out', 'Garden' or whatever command you intend to use and persist with. Do this a few times and the puppy will soon 'catch on', whereupon you will find that every time he wakes up he will stroll over to the garden door and attempt to get outside. This is fine, providing you are there to open the way for him. Do not blame him for a puddle if you are not! Obviously, you cannot expect him to go through the night without passing a motion, so line the floor of his abode, whether it is kennel or kitchen, with sheets of newspaper, which can be scooped up in the morning and quickly disposed of. Never forget to praise a puppy when he has done well, just as you should scold him for being stubborn and disobedient. Small puppies should never be chastised; it is likely to hurt their feelings, even affect their spirit. Worse, they lose confidence in the trainer and one so treated may well have such a set-back as to lose considerable ground in his training. A puppy should never be given food or drink just before he beds down for the night – no matter how late he retires. If you are training a puppy in the actual home, put him out into the garden just before you go to bed. This will give him an opportunity to do both his motions and sleep sounder through the hours which remain until morning.

Some owners prefer to restrict a puppy's movements at night so that any mess he makes during this time is confined to a fairly tight radius and not spread around the floor, making cleaning-up in the morning difficult and time consuming. A tea-chest makes a useful enclosure and it should be used open-end up. The puppy cannot climb out of it and its floor space of just in excess of three square feet can be well bedded down with absorbent newspaper or woodwool with a dry blanket on top. The puppy will be able to snuggle up in one corner with plenty of room to pass any motions he pleases out of his own way. Oddly enough, because he cannot wander in such a box, he is unlikely to make as much mess as if he had the full run of a kitchen floor. If the night is cold, install a stone hot water bottle wrapped in cloth for safety. The warmth and 'company' this affords will encourage the puppy to settle down and sleep through the night without crying and whimpering. However, should he make a noise on the first few nights, try and ignore him. It is unwise to keep coming down to comfort and soothe him, for he will take advantage of your compassion. Best leave him to cry and within a night or two he will have become used to it all.

ON THE LEAD

A small puppy seldom takes kindly to his first collar. It is best to buy a cheap strap leather or plastic collar and put it on him for progressively longer periods each day until he becomes used to wearing it and does not try to scratch it off. Once it has been accepted the collar can be put on occasionally but never during his sleeping hours as it will only 'ruff' the coat on his neck. The new lead should be also of the cheapest, lightest kind, but make sure it is strong enough to hold him.

Initial work in getting the puppy to move freely on collar and lead should be confined to the garden or at least some quiet place free from noise and other distractions. At first, he will want to pull out in front or drag back behind. He may be scared at what is going on and require some reassurance. This will have to take the form of gentle persuasion, encouragement – even bribery, using a few tasty titbits after the style of the carrot and donkey system if he seems loath to move forward. Reward co-operation with praise but do not spend too much time initially with the training, ten minutes being enough to start with, gradually increasing the period as the pupil shows aptitude and gets to enjoy the routine.

THE CHECK CORD

The check cord system is the best for teaching a puppy to come when called. The average small puppy when released from his lead will bound off, plunging at the nearest human or dog and getting into incalculable mischief. He will turn a deaf ear to his owner's every call and plea to return. This can prove frustrating to an owner and if allowed to continue unchecked will produce in the youngster a chronic state of indifference to command, which will be difficult to correct later. Tie a light check cord of some ten or twelve feet – longer, if you think you can manage it, to the puppy's collar. Shorten its length in your hand and walk out in much the same way as if you had the puppy on a normal length of lead. As the puppy moves eagerly ahead gradually let the line run out, *almost* to its full length, then call the puppy by name – 'Bob – Come!'. If he turns back to your side, reward him at once, but if he continues his rush away, call again 'Bob – Come!' allowing him just enough time before the line goes taut to return to you. If he refuses, the cord itself will check him within another second, probably bringing him over on to his back with a jerk. He will not like this for it will startle him and as the exercise is continued he will learn to expect this unpleasant tug as soon as he hears your voice. The call will cause him to hesitate, become alert and eventually halt, then return on command. When he has properly absorbed the lesson it can be continued without the cord.

Exercise

The Cocker Spaniel is basically and essentially an outdoor dog – he enjoys the open field and is clearly in his element where hedgerow and covert abounds. Bad weather means nothing to him, his flat, glossy coat keeping his skin dry in even the fiercest downpour of rain. To keep him fit he must have plenty of regular and daily exercise and he must never be deprived of this, even when outside conditions are bad. A sporting dog like this must be brought into hard, muscular condition and well up on his feet if he is to look good, work well and thrive in good health. To achieve this, walk him constantly on the lead over rough terrain such as gravel and cinder track paths, never allowing him to pull against the lead, as this is liable to throw out his shoulders and spoil his gait. Occasionally, let him run free in an open field or park where he is safe and away from traffic, throwing a ball or rubber ring for him to pursue and retrieve. Cast a ball up the side of a hill or slope to induce him in the valuable exercise of clambering which will help to develop his hindquarters. Once his permanent teeth are intact persuade him to swing off the ground on a suspended rubber tyre or firmly held stick; this will strengthen his neck muscles and develop the foreparts. Never over-exercise a dog, especially a puppy – bicycle pacing being a particularly poor and possibly ill-advised substitute for normal lead walking. A dog should be encouraged to look forward to his daily outing and the wise owner will ensure that his dog is taken where he can alert his mind with incidents and have pleasant surroundings. This will help to promote his appetite, thereby promoting good health and happiness.

Swimming

The Cocker Spaniel is a natural swimmer, water-shy dogs in this breed being rare. Should you have one which seems diffident about entering the water he can be encouraged in by throwing a stick or ball for him to retrieve or by employing another dog who enjoys the water and will show yours what to do. Although the Cocker is hardy in the field, it is best to rub him down after his dip, especially where his underparts and groins and armpits are concerned.

Guarding the home

Cockers are normally friendly dogs and some take an appreciable time before they develop any useful guarding ability, evincing even a little nervousness up to a late puppy stage. However, this should soon pass off and the dog will become more closely aware of strangers and unusual happenings around the house, giving tongue readily should the occasion demand. If he seems reluctant to bark when required to, you can encourage him by making various 'woofing' noises yourself, just when you note his attention has been alerted by a strange noise. He will probably 'parrot' the noise and once this has been tried successfully a few times the lesson will have been learned. However, the dog should not be allowed to bark continually without apparent reason, a habit which can annoy you as well as your neighbours. In effect praise and reward him when he guards correctly, scold and check him when he does not.

Training for farmstock

Most dogs brought up on pastoral land from puppyhood have become used to livestock and will ignore cattle, sheep and chickens, etc., being as one with them. However, a town dog suddenly introduced to the pungent and interesting odour of farm animals often becomes excited, rushing among them causing panic which may well culminate in an accident for which he is either shot or his owner is made responsible. A Cocker, while not especially prone to this should be taught to be tractable with domestic stock and taken among the animals while still a small puppy. His lead can be extended soon to a long cord, checking him meanwhile if he behaves too boisterously or shows signs of over-familiarity. Later he can be allowed to run free among the cattle, etc., making sure his presence does not bother them. Should he misbehave he must be returned to the leash and the lessons continued until he is quite trained.

Trials

The Kennel Club has stringent Rules and Regulations governing the conduct of Field Trials and Obedience Tests. The first Working Field Trials in which Spaniels could officially compete were held at Sutton Scarsdale estate in 1899. This was due to the work of the then Sporting Spaniel Club (later the Sporting Spaniel Society) who implemented thereby an idea evolved by the Spaniel Club of the day. The event referred to came thirty-five years after Pointers and Setters had held the first-ever Field Trial in Bedfordshire. The judges for the Sporting Spaniel Club were Mr W. Arkwright, on whose estate the Trials were held, and Mr Elias Bishop. Only two Stakes were staged – an 'All Age' Stake in which ten competed and a 'Puppy' Stake with four entrants. In spite of this small response, the event was much talked-about and enthusiasm soon grew, more ambitous Trials being envisaged as it became clear the idea was one to benefit the Spaniel. Up to this period controversy existed as to a Spaniel's specific duties in the field. In comparison with breeds such as the Setter and Pointer, the Spaniel is more a general purpose worker, his duties being diverse and his nature versatile. It is well-known that the Cocker Spaniel is generally employed to work in close liaison with the sportsman, to quest for game, flush it and retrieve when called upon to do so.

Because of this, it was difficult to lay down hard and fast rules to produce a standard of work at Field Trials. Clearly, this was one of the reasons which accounted for the Spaniel's relatively late entry into Field Trial work.

Field Trials exercise not only a healthy influence on the dogs and their owners, but serve to achieve one of the most important essentials in dogdom – that is the preservation of a breed's use and its temperament. Today too many breeds are losing their ability to do the job they were bred for. Few Pembroke Corgis can perform their age-old function of 'heeling' cattle; not many Collies, in spite of their attained magnificence, would know how to herd sheep. Certainly, no Staffordshire Bull Terrier today will get a chance to indulge himself at Bull-baiting, the pastime for which he was evolved. Gundogs and field dogs generally are fortunate in that their inherent abilities can be maintained at a high standard. This is particularly important in modern times when the trend is mainly for 'beauty' and to win prizes at dog shows. Every Cocker owner should endeavour to encourage working ability in his good-looking dog – only by so doing will he keep his breed at its present high level of competency in the field. Of course, there are many individuals bred today who could never prove themselves in Field Trial work, lacking the essential combination of steadiness and instinctive game-finding. However, if care is taken in the selection of foundation stock from bloodlines which have contributed to producing both field and show work winners, a good chance of success in both spheres will be achieved. Further, you will be assured of a fascinating and useful pursuit which cannot be bettered in the world of dogs.

Obviously, the basis on which training depends is obedience. It is important however, to ensure that not only the trainee, but the trainer enjoys the lessons as well as the exercise. A dog who has come from a sound line of field trained dogs reacts better, as a rule, to instruction than one whose ancestry is limited mainly to showbench stock. The best age to start a puppy is when he is about four months old and with a fairly confident outlook. A shy Cocker might mean starting later with, but he should not be eliminated from your training plans as very often such a dog when he settles down makes a sensitive pupil.

The initial work with a small puppy is to get him to respond to his name and to a whistle recall, later to retrieve some small object or 'dummy'. This can take the form of a sock or glove or rabbit skin. Throw the object a few yards ahead of the pupil; he will run to it and pick it up. Call him by name and encourage him to bring it back to the hand. A lot of puppies will at first think this is fine game and attempt to rush off with the prize. A culprit must be checked in this from the outset and an effective method of encouragement is to move away from him, calling his name. He will then move with you, probably alongside your tracks and you can reach down and gently remove the dummy from his mouth. On doing this, reward him with verbal praise and a pat or two on the head, but avoid giving him titbits. With a few more lessons he should become fairly adept at sighting and retrieving an object. The next lesson should be to encourage him to use his nose, working in the 'rough'. Throw the dummy so that it falls to the ground in light cover out of sight. The Spaniel will soon learn to locate it then retrieve. This lesson should be of short duration as a puppy can soon get bored and tired and lose interest in the instruction.

The next stage is to get the youngsters to drop on command and to remain until ordered to move. The lesson should commence with the puppy on his lead so that trainer and dog are as a unit. This will discourage the dog from wandering and being distracted by outside influences. Walk him a short way, then give sharp command 'Drop!' at the same time halting and pressing the dog down gently but firmly on his haunches. He should remain there for a moment or two then be allowed to rise and move forward. The following step is to get him into the dropped position, remaining there while the trainer walks on ahead away from him. He may try to rise and follow the trainer in which case he should be returned immediately to the exact spot he has just vacated, pressed down into and told to remain. Persistency and repetition without tiring the puppy will soon have their effect and the pupil will soon drop at command or whistle or a hand signal from his trainer. Never continue the lesson for too long – ten minute lessons twice a day will usually prove sufficient and by the time two weeks have passed the average intelligent puppy will be showing considerable promise. The puppy must learn to retrieve the dummy on command from the dropped position, a short waiting period being insisted upon before he is told to 'Fetch!' Sometimes an eager pupil will attempt to run in before the command is given. Such a tendency must be checked at once. The next step is to train him to drop at a distance. The instructor will give the command to drop, then walk on ahead for about twenty yards. He will then call the dog up, waiting until the puppy is fairly near to him, whereupon he will issue the command to drop. As the puppy shows promise at this, a number of drops can be called-for in the run up, until he is quite proficient. A check cord can be employed if required, but this is preferred for rather slow learners and if possible dispense with it, especially if the dog is a little nervous as it will unsettle him. If however, it becomes necessary to use one, it should be pulled up with a jerk as the word of command is given, the puppy soon learning to sit. The Spaniel must always be ready to come to heel on the trainer's left side. This means training him initially on a short lead, then if he pulls forward the command 'Heel!' should be given and the lead jerked back. Later, when he responds at once to the verbal command he can be allowed to run free with the lead trailing behind him. The latter can then be trodden on to check the dog if he moves too far forward.

Early training to gunfire is essential. The first introduction to the sound is best made by getting a colleague to fire a charge at some distance from the kennel or pound where the dog is eating, the trainer standing by meanwhile. Immediately, the sound is heard give the command 'Drop!' which the puppy should obey in spite of the meal's attraction. Continue the lesson daily, each time firing a charge a little nearer to where the dog stands, delivering the command to drop at the same time, until the gun can be fired almost over the puppy's head. Soon, the youngster will learn to drop every time the report is heard – this he must do if he is to make a good gundog.

Not many young Spaniels learn how to use their nose until they reach the age of six months. By this age he will have at least some knowledge of field atmosphere – but steadiness is something he will acquire with experience. For the average man, a simple method of getting his Cocker used to game and to control his temptation is to walk him round a penned tame rabbit, checking him when he lunges at the creature – which should be out of harm's way. He will soon learn that the rabbit is not to be chased, when he can be released and allowed to approach it, giving the command to drop as the animal moves away from him. Soon, when he shows signs of steadiness he must be got used to real game. The 'dummy' used in this early training can be replaced with a 'cold' bird or rabbit, the dog being sent back for it from a forward position. Later, a freshly shot bird can be introduced and the training stepped up in this way. If the initial lessons he received were properly absorbed he will respond well to it all, but no surprise need be felt if the pupil loiters with a warm bird. This can often be remedied by the trainer moving away sharply from the scene, calling the dog by name.

There is plenty to interest and distract a young puppy from his training when he is taken into the field. However, his instinct will usually stand him in good stead and cause him to shape up to proper application to the job. The best thing that could happen to him on his first day out is for a rabbit to break-away in front of him so that you can give the command to drop. Assuming he does this, he is showing promise and he should be left in the dropped position for a rather longer time than usual. To emphasise the need for steadiness, then work him in the opposite direction to that taken by the rabbit. However, if he is diverse and attempts to chase the rabbit, try and forestall him or wait for his return; place him exactly on the vacated drop position, showing your displeasure.

Quartering is an important feature of the Spaniel's field work and most individuals are good at it. The dog should be trained to work no more than twenty-five yards away from the trainer, quartering systematically from side to side, covering the ground without missing game. As soon as he has reached the limit of his range, he can be whistled to drop then waved to the opposite side of the trainer. When working in the field, a whistle is probably better than a vocal command as it is less likely to disturb the game.

A sound training is usually effected when two people are available on the shoot itself – one to do the shooting and the trainer to concentrate on the dog. His training at this stage is very important and both patience and understanding will have to be employed to bring him to perfection. Not every shot indicates a retrieve and this is not easy for a young dog to comprehend, especially when he is not despatched for everything which is down. As he gets to understand his work better he can be allowed after a 'runner' or wounded game. He should be dropped before every retrieve and the sportsman should always re-load first before despatching the dog. A dog allowed out immediately may run into shot and it is often necessary to sacrifice some good shooting at times for the sake of training a first-class worker. It is most important that dog and man work well together and with confidence. Never chastise or punish a dog unless he knows why you are annoyed with him. You need his respect to get the best from him and he needs your appreciation if he is to work well for you. Lastly, never work a dog who is tired, bored or 'off colour'.

The title of Field Trial Champion is the entitlement of a Cocker Spaniel who has either won the Cocker Spaniel Championship Stake or has won two first prizes at two different Field Trials in Open or All-Aged Stakes for Cocker Spaniels or open to any variety of Spaniel. These wins will not qualify if there are more than 32 runners at a two-day meeting or more than 16 runners at a one-day meeting (Brace and Team Stakes excluded).

Those interested in this fascinating work with Spaniels should obtain a copy of Kennel Club Field Trial Rules from The Kennel Club office in London.

WORKING TRIALS AND OBEDIENCE TESTS

Although not so popular with the Spaniel family as Field Trials, the increasing number of Obedience Trials being held give evidence as to the public's attitude to these tests of intelligence and adaptability. Working Trials, like the ordinary Dog Shows are divided into three main categories – Championship, Open and Members' events. Obedience shows are frequently held in conjunction with Dog Shows or a Working Trials event or commonly as an individual fixture. No bitch in season is allowed to compete at these functions. (Working Trial Rules and

Obedience Classes Rules in the *Year Book*, price £1.00 from The Kennel Club office.)

WORKING TRIAL CHAMPION

The Kennel Club awards its Working Trial Certificate to any dog winning an Open Stake at a Championship Working Trial, provided it has obtained 70 per cent or more marks as indicated in the Schedule of Points in the appropriate columns for each group of exercises separately shown in that Schedule and has also been awarded the qualification 'Excellent' by obtaining at least 80 per cent of the possible total of marks for the Stake.

A dog shall qualify for the title of Working Trial Champion if he is awarded two Kennel Club Working Trial Certificates by different judges at Championship Working Trials duly licensed by the Committee of The Kennel Club as Championship fixtures.

DEFINITIONS OF STAKES

It should be noted that wins at Members' Working Trials do not count when a dog enters for Championship or Open Working Trials and any dog entered in *P.D. or *T.D. Stakes shall not be eligible to enter in any other Stake.

QUALIFICATIONS FOR CHAMPIONSHIP AND OPEN WORKING TRIALS

Stake	*Championship*	*Open*
COMPANION DOG (C.D.)	For dogs which have not won three or more first prizes in C.D. Stakes or any prize in any other Stake at Championship Working Trials.	For dogs which have not won three or more first prizes in C.D. Stakes or any prize in U.D. Stakes, W.D. Stakes, P.D. or T.D. Stakes at Open or Championship Working Trials.
ALL BREEDS UTILITY DOG (U.D.)	For dogs which have won a Certificate of Merit in a U.D. Stake. A dog is not eligible for entry in this Stake if it has been entered in the W.D. Stakes on the same day.	For dogs which have not been awarded a Certificate of Merit in U.D., W.D., P.D. or T.D. Stakes.
WORKING DOG (W.D.)	For dogs which have qualified U.D. Ex. and have won a Certificate of Merit in W.D. Stakes.	For dogs which have been awarded a Certificate of Merit in U.D. Stakes but not in W.D., P.D., or T.D. Stakes.

With acknowledgements to the Kennel Club for their permission to reproduce the Regulations for Working Trials and Obedience Tests.
*Police Dog and Tracking Dog with which categories we are not concerned here.

SCHEDULE OF POINTS

COMPANION DOG (CD) STAKE

Description of Exercises and Individual Marks	Group Total	Min. Group Qual. Mark

Group I. Control

1. Heel on Leash   5
   On the handler's command 'Heel', the dog should follow as closely as possible to the left knee of the handler, who should walk smartly in his normal and natural manner. Any tightening or jerking of the leash, or any act, signal or command which, in the opinion of the Judges gives the dog unnecessary or unfair assistance, shall be penalised. The exercise consists of 'left turns', 'right turns', 'about turns', and marching in the 'figure of eight' at normal walking pace between objects or people two yards apart. The Judge may, at his discretion, test also at a fast or very slow pace.

2. Heel Free   10
   (This should be executed as in No. 1 except that the dog is off the leash.)

3. Recall to Handler   5
   The dog should be recalled from the 'down' or sitting position, the handler being as far as possible from the dog at the discretion of the Judge. The dog should return at a smart pace and sit in front of the handler, afterwards going smartly to heel on command or signal; handler to await command of the Judge.

4. Sending the dog away   10
   In the direction indicated by the Judge not less than 20 yards and dropping on order from Judge to handler. The dog should drop instantly and remain down until the Judge instructs the handler to call his dog up.   30   21

Group II. Stays

5. Sit (two minutes)   10

The dogs shall sit for the full period of two minutes, all the handlers being out of sight as far as possible from the dogs at the Judge's discretion. On the handlers' return to their dogs the latter should not move from the sitting position until the Judge's permission has been given. All dogs shall be tested together, sufficient Stewards being detailed to assist. The Judges may cause the dogs to be tested by sending Stewards to walk among them during the exercise.

6. Down 10 minutes, handler out of sight   10

The dog must remain in the lying down position for the full period specified, the handler being out of sight until ordered to return by the Judge. The dog should not rise from the 'down' position until the Judge declares the exercise complete. The Judge may cause a dog to be tested by sending Stewards to walk around it during the exercise.   20   14

Group III. Agility

7. (a) Scale Jump – (3); Stay – (2); and recall over scale –
       (5)   10

    Dogs not exceeding 10 in. at shoulder – 3 ft.
    Dogs not exceeding 15 in. at shoulder – 4 ft.
    Dogs *exceeding* 15 in. at shoulder – 6 ft.

  (b) Clear Jump   5

    Dogs not exceeding 10 in. at shoulder – 1 ft. 6 in.
    Dogs not exceeding 15 in. at shoulder – 2 ft.
    Dogs *exceeding* 15 in. at shoulder – 3 ft.

  (c) Long Jump   5

    Dogs not exceeding 10 in. at shoulder – 4 ft.
    Dogs not exceeding 15 in. at shoulder – 6 ft.
    Dogs *exceeding* 15 in. at shoulder – 9 ft.   20   14

Group IV. Retrieving and Nose

8. Retrieving a Dumb-bell on the flat   10

The dog shall not move forward to retrieve nor deliver to hand on return until ordered by the handler on the Judge's instructions. The retrieve should be executed at a fast trot or gallop without mouthing or playing with the object. After delivery the dog should return to heel.

9. Elementary Search   20
   Controlled Search of an area foiled ground to find and
   retrieve one Judge's article with handler's scent,
   placed by Steward, unseen by dog and handler. This
   area should be approximately 12 yards square and the
   time allowed 2 minutes. A separate area to be allowed
   for each dog. Handler must remain outside the area
   although allowed to move.   30   21

                                     TOTAL   100   70

ALL BREEDS UTILITY DOG (UD) STAKE

	Group Total	Min. Group Qual. Mark
Group I. Control		
1. Heel Free 5		
2. Sending dog away not less than 20 yards and dropping on order from Judge to handler 10		
3. Retrieving dumb-bell of handler's choice on the flat 5		
4. Long Down 10 min., handler out of sight 10		
5. Steadiness to Gunshot 5	35	25
Group II. Agility		
6. (a) Scale (3); Stay (2); and recall over Scale (5) 10		
Dogs not exceeding 10 in. at shoulder – 3 ft.		
Dogs not exceeding 15 in. at shoulder – 4 ft.		
Dogs *exceeding* 15 in. at shoulder – 6 ft.		
(b) Clear Jump 5		
Dogs not exceeding 10 in. at shoulder – 1 ft. 6 in.		
Dogs not exceeding 15 in. at shoulder – 2 ft.		
Dogs *exceeding* 15 in. at shoulder – 3 ft.		
(c) Long Jump 5		
Dogs not exceeding 10 in. at shoulder – 4 ft.		
Dogs not exceeding 15 in. at shoulder – 6 ft.		
Dogs *exceeding* 15 in. at shoulder – 9 ft. —	20	14

Group III. Nosework

7. Search. Controlled search of an area of foiled ground
   to find and retrieve four strange articles handled and
   placed by some person other than the handler. The
   area should be fresh for each dog and approximately
   25 yards square and the time allowed five minutes.

Two articles must be found. (See item F in the 'Notes for the Guidance of Judges and Competitors')   35

8. Leash Track. Not less than ½-mile long and at least ½-hour old on track laid as far as possible by a stranger to the dog. The tracklayer's article to be left at the end of the track. One peg, not more than 30 yards from the commencement of the track will be left to indicate the direction of the track.

One recast will be allowed at the discretion of the Judge (see item I(a) in 'Notes for the Guidance of Judges and Competitors').

For the track   95
For recognition of article by the dog   15   145   102

TOTAL   200   141

WORKING DOG (WD) STAKE

Description of Exercises and Individual Marks		Group Total	Min. Group Qual. Marks

Group I. Control

1. Heel free   5
2. Sending dog away not less than 20 yards and dropping on order from Judge to Handler   10
3. Retrieving dumb-bell of handler's choice on the flat 5
4. Long Down 10 min., handler out of sight   10
5. Steadiness to Gunshot   5

—   35   25

Group II. Agility

6. (a) 6 ft. Scale – (3); Stay – (2); and recall over Scale (5)   10
   (b) Clear Jump – 3 ft.   5
   (c) Long Jump – 9 ft.   5

—   20   14

Group III. Nosework

7. Search. Controlled search of an area of foiled ground to find and retrieve four strange articles handled and placed by some person other than the handler. The area should be fresh for each dog and approximately

25 yards square and the time allowed five minutes. Two articles must be found. (See item F in the 'Notes for the Guidance of Judges and Competitors'.)   35

8. Leash Track. There should be no recasts in the direction of the Judge. The Track should be not less than $\frac{1}{2}$-mile long and at least $1\frac{1}{2}$-hours old. Two different kinds of article will be dropped on the track, similar articles to be used by each tracklayer and readily identifiable by him. One article must be found to qualify. (See Item I(b) in 'Notes for the Guidance of Judges and Competitors'.)

For the track   90

For recognition of two articles by the dog (10 points each)   20   145   102

TOTAL   200   141

6 Management and Care

A dog thrives well on proper feeding, exercise and understanding. When these and other essentials exist, the animal becomes well primed as a good companion and is usually a happy one.

An owner should study the functioning of his Cocker's mind. Quite apart from the benefit to be gained in his training (discussed in the previous chapter), he can be managed better and more effectively to suit his particular temperament. The way a dog is treated, the atmosphere of the home in which he lives, has a good deal of effect on temperament and behaviour and he will respond to the moods of those with whom he is in daily contact. It is important when handling and managing dogs to exercise consistency. It is no good saying and doing one thing one day, then altering your methods the next. If you do, the dog will never get to know what you really want of him.

So often when small puppies rush around the home, boisterous and out of control, it seems amusing; but as a dog matures such habits become far from funny! This is why it is important to get a dog used to a management routine right from puppyhood. In fact, even a two month old puppy should become used to calculated management from the time he enters his new owner's home.

Chewing

Some puppies when left alone become bored and start to chew at the nearest thing. They seldom discriminate between objects which are valuable or worthless and if the article concerned falls into the former category, it is usually the owner's fault for leaving it there! A puppy can have no way of differentiating between the two and when he has to be left to his own devices he should be given something safe to chew upon. Should he prove a compulsive chewer, i.e. rushes at furniture and hanging curtains as soon as he sees them, scold him and deposit him firmly on his bed or in a box out of the way. He will soon learn.

Bathing

Whereas the average Cocker enjoys a swim, he takes much less kindly to being bundled into a bath and soaped all over! This is a job, which although necessary at times should be conducted with minimal fuss. A dog should be saved from being scared and irritated and providing you make a point of getting all your dog bath paraphernalia to hand before you start, the amount of fuss will be negligible. You will need two good sized terry bath towels, one to remove surplus moisture, the other to dry off afterwards. If you can prepare three receptacles, one with ready-made shampoo, the other two filled with warm water rinses, the operation can be speeded up. A good sized chamois leather will be found useful to finish off with and produce a nice gloss on the dog's coat. Use a small face cloth for wiping round the eyes, ears and face generally, which in any case should be left until last. Before putting the dog into the bath, place a flat rubber mat on the bottom; this will prevent him slipping about during the ablutions. Make sure the bath water is only just warm, never hot for that is bad for a dog's skin. Ensure that his coat has been thoroughly combed through to remove any tangling and place him gently in the water. Steady him with one hand, pouring a bowl of warm water over his body with the other. Avoid dousing the head at this stage, then working from the rear end, go up the body working in the shampoo from the container you have prepared. Once a good lather has been developed and the dirt is seen coming out, rinse with clear warm water from one of your nearby receptacles. Finally, deal with the head, using the small face square for more gentle application to make sure no soap enters the dog's eyes, ears and under the lips. Then rinse slowly with your final container of clear water. If possible, at this stage the dog should be allowed a good shake, which will dispose at once of all the surplus moisture. Then towel down the coat carefully with one of the terry towels. This will soon get wet, when you can use the second towel to dry off up to the point when you introduce the chamois leather or electric hairdryer. The former is preferable as it not only finishes off well but will not brittle the coat such as hot air might.

Make sure the dog's skin is quite dry and pay particular attention to drying his underparts, groins, genitals, arm-pits and anal region, not forgetting between the toes. If you have used cotton wool ear-plugs to protect the inner ears, remove these and wipe off any greasy eye-protecting preparations employed. Before releasing him after his bath, comb his coat well and then brush down generally, completing the grooming. Keep him in an even temperature until you are quite sure as to his overall dryness.

No dog should be bathed more than is absolutely necessary and when brushing and combing will suffice, it is better, for soap will remove the natural oils from a dog's coat, making it dull and lifeless for some days.

Mrs V. Hillary's
Hi-Fidelity of
Bidston

CHAMBERS

Grooming

A Cocker needs patient and constant attention to his coat, not only to
keep it healthy and clean and to tone up his circulation and muscles, but
to maintain good general appearance. Most breeders, apart from daily
combing and brushing to prevent matting, attend to their Cockers three
or four times a week. They will check the eyes, always indicative of a
dog's general health and the ears to remove wax and foreign bodies
picked up in the fields as well as the lips for ulceration. The teeth and
gums should be checked and the tail lifted to make sure the area below is
clean, the anal glands needing especially to be in healthy condition. Even
the cleanest kept dogs pick up fleas and lice occasionally, so check

Ms J. Walker's Okell Ovett

through to the skin for these. They usually conglomerate around the tail set-on, so look here first, rubbing back the coat with your thumb. If resident, some may be picked out with the fingers, but a good dusting of proprietary flea powder is best. Make sure the feathering behind the legs is kept within reasonable bounds. The most effective way to remove any unwanted profusion is to pluck it manually. Clippers and knives never achieve such a finished look and one soon gets adept at the former method.

A Cocker youngster usually starts to shed his coat several months before he reaches the yearling stage. Care should be taken to remove all the old hair as it is noted; this will prevent an unpleasant shaggy appearance developing. Keep the feet free from superfluous hair, using snub-nosed scissors to trim it away carefully from between the toes and pads, a procedure usually necessary about once a month. The same type of scissors should be used for paring the toenails if they are too long, although it is better to keep these short by regular exercising on rough ground like gravel paths and cinder tracks. If the nails must be cut, take care that you do not cut too close into the quick. This will produce not only bleeding, but considerable pain to the dog and may well make him fearful and unco-operative of any future administrations to his feet.

As most experienced exhibitors are aware, there is an art in grooming which can and often does, make all the difference to whether a dog wins

D. and S. Telford's
Sh. Ch. Courtmaster
Je Suis

first prize or not! Obviously, it is nice from an aesthetic viewpoint to see a well-groomed Cocker, but if a dog is to gain maximum marks in the 'General Appearance' section of the breed Standard, he must look good. Admittedly, cunning grooming is sometimes contrived to beguile a judge, and often it does from a mere visual assessment. However, only an incompetent adjudicator would continue to be duped once he had manually inspected such an exhibit.

Trimming

Mrs E. S. Robertson and her daughter of the famous 'Nostrebor' Cocker kennels recommend the following system of trimming the breed. All

Cockers should be treated as individuals. When dealing with a puppy, it is best to wait for the coat to show signs of coming out naturally before starting to help it manually. No coat should be eased out of a puppy before it is ready to come.

It is a good idea to place before you a picture of a well-trimmed and well-prepared Cocker, so you have a guide to work to. Stand the dog on a table which has a rough surface as no dog likes slipping about when he is being trimmed. Keep a lead on him so that you have something to grab if he becomes fidgety. Support him underneath to keep him in a standing position and brush and comb him all over. Start the trimming at his rear end. This will get him used to the situation and he will not be frightened. With a good sweep to the line of stifle in mind, shape the hair down on

K. and S. Morrisson's Sh. Ch. Kendra Harmony Child

the front of the hind leg. Stand behind the dog, lift up his tail and take the hair short to where the feathering falls downwards. Tidy the hair to the top of the hock to the pad, but not too close or it will detract from the well boned effect of the dog. Trim the hair short on both sides of the tail and tidy the hair off at the tail extremity. Trimming scissors can be used for this, but other cutting instruments may well ruin a dog's coat irreparably.

Starting at the rear foot, take the hair short on both sides of the foot, not going beyond the side of the nails. With the weight on the foot cut the hair back only to the middle of the nail, then push the hair up between the toes and shape it carefully. On no account cut the hair from between the toes as this gives a 'starfish' effect instead of the desired 'cat-foot' required by the breed Standard. The front feet are usually more difficult than the back feet and can only be done properly after some practice. About every fifteen minutes take the dog off the table and stand him in front of a mirror, studying the effect of your labours. At this stage, you could give him a short walk to relieve his boredom.

With many Cockers there is a profusion of hair over the ribs and down the sides. This must be reduced by *plucking*, easing a few hairs out at a time. You will find that if you rub a little chalk into the hair it will come out easier. Push the soft hair up and by holding the skin in your left hand, pull the hair out with your right, making sure you do not hurt the dog, of course. Trim the hair down from the elbow to the middle of the back leg in a straight line. The elbow of the front leg should be inconspicuous and there is a natural line where the feathering falls backwards. All hair in front of this should be taken short. A common mistake is to think that the feathering at the back of the foot should be taken off about two inches from the ground. This will do no more than to give an appearance of flat pasterns and big feet. The feathering should be allowed to fall naturally to the ground level. Carefully trim the feathering so that the pastern bone is hidden.

All surplus hair on neck and shoulders should be plucked to give a clean line, remembering that the *natural* fall of the hair should be followed, and this at all times. All hair on the top-knot must be pulled out, pushing the soft hair up and pulling out only a few hairs at a time without hurting the dog. Pluck out the hair about one-third of the way down the ear-flap until the hair is flat – then comb the fringes very thoroughly right down to the skin.

Many people think they brush and comb their dog thoroughly, whereas in fact they do little more than just 'tickle the top of the mat'. Lift up the ear and carefully cut off all the hair sticking out, taking great care to ensure that the dog does not jerk his head suddenly and get cut. Take particular care of the small fold on the side of the ear flap. Lice and fleas, if they are present, are bound to be present here. Hold the dog's head up and his ears back and clip from the corner of the ear to the 'Adam's apple' along the natural growth line of the hair ten days before you intend to show him. Then pluck the rest of the hair out down to the breastbone, cleaning out along the natural line then taking it short when going towards the elbows. Any facial whiskers must be removed, either pulled (when possible) or cut off.

Matting will often be found under the hindquarters, elbows and ears, and these three places should be brushed meticulously. If they become badly matted, the mats can sometimes he removed without actually spoiling the dog's appearance, but this is more a job for the experienced person. Mud clots under the feet can prove both painful and distressing, and some dogs will try to remove them by gnawing and biting. The clots should be cut away carefully from under the pads, putting the scissors in the front corner of the rear pad of the foot from either side, snipping very carefully and slowly between skin and the mat.

It can take as much as five years practice to learn the art of trimming correctly. The process requires patience and a close regard for the animal being prepared. The average dog, while not liking the business of manhandling, will always respond to understanding, care and kindness.

Kennelling

If you own just one dog, then he is better kept in the home. There he will thrive well, learn your ways as well as those of the family and make a useful guard as well as a pleasant companion. Left alone in a restricted garden kennel he will live a life no better than a prisoner in solitary confinement and his intelligence, happiness as well as his use to you will suffer considerably.

However, where a number of dogs are owned, it becomes necessary to provide proper kennel facilities. Both systems are discussed herewith:

Indoor: Most animals, and dogs are no exception, like to lay claim to their own territory. Your Cocker should have an accepted position for his bed, his meals and water bowl. His bed (The 'Goddard' bed made of metal hinged framework and canvas is very good) should be such a size that he can lie comfortably snug in it without being cramped. Hygiene is most important – the blanket should be shaken out every morning and replaced not less than once a week, the bed itself being disinfected at regular intervals. Many people allow their dogs to sleep in the kitchen, which being often a tiled room is easy to keep clean. The Cocker with his warm coat is unlikely to feel cold very much, but on cold nights he will appreciate the extra warmth provided by a stove or central heating. The main thing to avoid with dogs is a draught, for this can cause sickness and general debility. Ensure that he sleeps a little off ground level or in a box with raised sides all round.

Outdoor: Many kinds of good kennels are available today, from ordinary 'one-dog' affairs to extensive ranges, all carefully designed by experts. There are indoor kennels too, but Cockers are too big for these, requiring plenty of floor space, at least five square feet per dog. This applies to sleeping and enclosure accommodation only, a wired-in run being an essential adjunct. Too much sleeping room will prevent the dog warming it up with his body heat in cold weather, too little will cramp him. When you buy the kennel make sure it is high enough to stand up in. One cannot cope effectively in a bent double position and a well-planned kennel should be self-contained, each dog being easily accessible yet unable to physically contact another inmate. At the end of the range a small locker should be erected where sawdust, woodwool, shovel and disinfectants are readily available from an outside door. Of course, for a sick dog or whelping bitch it is essential that one kennel at least should be kept isolated from the main range. Every kennel should have its outside run at least the normal width of the compartment with as much length to it as you can manage. The floors of the run should be of concrete or of some recommended composition. Cinders are good, especially for keeping the pasterns firm, but these do not wash down nearly so well as smooth surfaces. Always face the kennel south or south-west away from the unpleasant winds of your district, raising the floor slightly from the ground to obviate dampness and allow air to circulate below. Fill in the gaps so made with close mesh wire netting to prevent puppies or small wild animals from crawling underneath. Rats are frequently a menace where dogs are kept. Apart from their personal unpleasantness, they bring in disease, especially the dreaded leptospirosis. At the first signs of these unwelcome visitors, action must be taken to exterminate them. Keep the kennels away from overhanging trees and foliage generally when it is likely to drip water on the dogs and prevent the free passage of air and sunlight.

Ordinary lighting and heating installation should be adequate for even the coldest snap. Most electricians will fix up an extension to the house supply for a nominal sum. Heating must be *safe*; it should be installed to start at kennel floor level so that the heat rises while maintaining a steady temperature where the dog sleeps. Electric tubular heating is popular with many breeders, several low consumption units especially designed for kennel use being available. Small paraffin heaters can be bought, but have the disadvantage of smelling as they age. In any case, these and all forms of heating should be ringed with a wire guard for safety beyond a dog's reach.

Punishment

Punishment to a dog should be meted out sparingly and with care. Applied psychology has usually better effect and a good scolding will achieve results with an animal of average intelligence. Should firmer action seem necessary, a tightly rolled-up newspaper often works wonders. It makes a disciplinary noise and yet does not hurt, usually startling a dog into obedience. After just a few administrations, the pupil will do what he is told merely at the sight of it.

No dog should be disciplined unless it has been made abundantly clear what his master has expected of him and how he has done wrong. An animal so unfairly treated usually loses confidence in his handler or at least is severely set back in normal progress.

How to sell

No breeder of sound, healthy and typical well-bred Cockers should find difficulty in placing his stock where, if good enough, it will be exhibited or at least appreciated in someone's family circle. The breed is very popular and the demand for quality stock is constant, sometimes exceeding the supply. Nevertheless, you are unlikely to sell your puppies unless you announce the fact that you have some and make an effort to dispose of those you do not wish to keep for yourself.

Some Cocker Spaniel kennels have such a call for well-bred youngsters that they have to buy in puppies for re-sale, their own home-bred stock being insufficient for their needs. Their interest will naturally be high in puppies which have emanated from the kennel's own particular strain. Therefore, it may prove worthwhile approaching the kennels from whom you purchased your bitch or the kennels associated with the stud dog you used to her. Of course, you are unlikely to reap as much return financially had you sold them piecemeal, but you should insist in your own interest on the kennel taking your litter *en bloc* as soon as it is ready to go. If only the best members are selected and taken you will be left with the mediocre, therefore less saleable stock on your hands.

As to some guide in the price to accept, you should ascertain the average price being asked for puppies bred and reared such as yours, preferably from the kennel you are selling to. Then you should try and negotiate a price which would show the sellers about 40–50 per cent gross profit on their cost after re-sale. When you realise that they have to spend valuable time interviewing and educating potential customers, pay for advertising which will draw in those customers, then bear the burden on heavy freight and transport bills, their net return is comparatively small. They will also have to attend to the various after-sales queries which are bound to crop up and in fact take full responsibility for these sales to their customers. This then, is a very straightforward and clean way of selling one's puppies and many small breeders like to dispose their stock in this manner. If it worries you where the puppies have gone to after being sold, you will find some kennel buyers will inform you their whereabouts, but failing this you can usually trace them through the registration and transfer columns of *The Kennel Gazette* monthly supplement. Of course, should you follow-up and check on the well-being of the puppies your approach should be discreet as the owners are not *your* customers and some will object to being quizzed, however well-meaning your intentions.

If you prefer to secure the maximum financial return for your puppies then you will have to do your own selling. You may be fortunate in having a Cocker Spaniel Club membership which allows you to take advantage of a system which will put you in touch with enquiring buyers for young stock. Apart from your club subscription which of course, will offer you many more facilities than this one, such an arrangement will cost you nothing. You can then deal with every enquiry as it comes in, giving the people details of your puppies' age, breeding, colours and price and/or presenting them in person to interested visitors. If the litter is too young to go immediately, you can reserve individual puppies in advance of their leaving age, which should be about ten weeks, but make sure you take a deposit from the buyer. A nominal sum is often sufficient to ensure that his desire to own a puppy is genuine and that he will not revoke at the eleventh hour, a situation which can prove very annoying if for a frivolous reason, as you would probably have been able to sell his puppy in the past few weeks several times over.

If you decide to advertise your stock the weekly dog journals *Dog World* and *Our Dogs* are best for these specialise strictly for those interested in dogs. *Exchange and Mart's* dog sale column is very effective too, and widely read by people with companion and exhibition stock in mind. If you have a telephone insert the number in your advertisement. Many will pick up a telephone and ring you whereas they might not be bothered to put pen to paper. Box numbers offering dogs are of little use – the average interested party having made up his mind to own a puppy wants it at once and cannot wait several days for a written reply. The national press is effective, the London *Evening Standard* being good especially on Friday evenings.

Make your advertisement succinct and informative. The buyer wants to know the breed, age, sexes and the colours of your puppies. He wants to know the price too of course, but sometimes it is prudent to keep this salient item from the advertisement, divulging it when you see him or start negotiating the sale. The reason for this is that many prospective buyers have little or no idea as to pedigree dog prices today, not realising what it costs to buy and rear dogs, mate them and bring on healthy properly presented puppies up to their going-away age. If you advertise in the dog papers, then some readers will want to know your puppies' breeding. A suitable framed advertisement of such journals is exampled as follows:

Mrs M. Robinson's
Craigleith Candyman

COCKER SPANIELS. Finest Pedigree breeding (Ch. .... ×
Ch. ....). Golden puppies both sexes 10 weeks old now.
Kennel Club registered. Sound and Healthy. Moderate Prices.
(Name, Address and Telephone Number.)

Never over-state. Effusive superlatives can make your intending buyer
suspicious, thereby achieving the opposite effect for which you had

hoped. Never promise too much either – to announce that your puppies will make 'big winners' may well leave you open to recrimination and attack later on when it is has been found perhaps that they could not win a thing! There is no harm in describing them as 'promising' or 'should be up to show standard' – such phrases are in good order so long as you believe them yourself. Naturally, it is up to you to ensure that your stock is sound and healthy and of factual pedigree breeding when you sell it. To fail in these simple tenets is unfair to the puppies and to the buyers and can involve you unpleasantly in difficuties and expense at a later date.

Care of the stud dog

The dog intended for regular use as a stud must be well cared for and maintained in perfect bloom. As a specimen of course, he needs not only to be of high order, but noble, full of type and masculinity but able to reproduce not only his own good features, but also the best from his ancestry. To be patronised by bitch owners seeking to improve their strains he must prove to their satisfaction that he is prepotent for no stud dog can impress any worthwhile mark on his breed unless he can lay claim to some outstanding sons and daughters.

The best time to let a young dog have his first bitch is when he is about a year old, many owners making it a rule to find him a mating when he reaches ten months. It is important however, that the dog should be quite well grown and in good health at the time and it is better if this first union is with a matron bitch. Her experience will make the service easier for him, young untried maiden bitches often proving coy and difficult when first mated. His second mating can take place about a month or two later and again just before he is eighteen months old. It is inadvisable to permit too many bitches to visit him in his first two years of life – as many a young dog has been spoilt by over-indulgence at stud. Of course, a lot depends on the individual, some dogs being much more virile and keen than others. However, generally speaking, three to four matings allowed up to his second birthday is a safe rule to adopt. The dog can then be gradually introduced to more frequent work after this time taking on about one bitch a week if he gets the chance. A dog at regular stud by the time he is three years old can manage perhaps more, but a heavily worked stud dog soon goes 'ragged' if his owner does not plough in to him plenty of good food and maintain him well with exercise. High-protein meals which include fresh, raw meat, eggs, white fish with the occasional teaspoonful of halibut-liver oil are essential. A dog will usually give some indication that his bodily health is failing under heavy stud duties by a falling-off of body weight, especially in the regions of loins and shoulders. His coat, usually in high bloom will become dull,

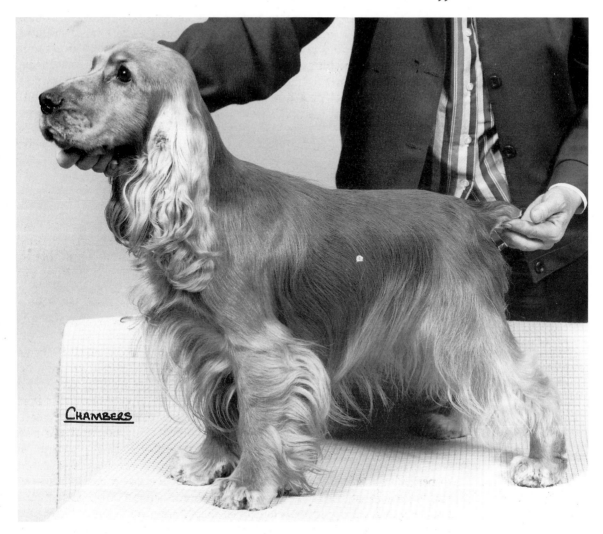

even staring. Should this be noted, his owner should rest him for at least a month, building him up meanwhile with good food. When he is ready to recommence at stud, his services should be relegated to a few selected bitches until it seems he is able to resume normal work. Should it be observed that a stud dog is diffident in his courtship but seems otherwise in good physical shape, check on his genitals. It may be that some soreness exists from an earlier mating or that the sheath is not resting comfortably. Always make a point of examining him underneath after every mating to ensure that he is at ease and if necessary, sponge the area with a weak solution of antiseptic for hygiene.

Mrs V. Hillary's Triciamar Topical of Bidston

The average healthy stud can serve bitches at the rate of three or four a month up to the age of six years, but after this the number should be halved, then curtailed severely during the latter years of life. Much depends on how *regularly* the dog has been used as to how long he is allowed to keep going at his work. No elderly dog should be permitted to serve a bitch if he has been rested off from stud work for a long period previously.

Rescue Service

This is a humane service of rehabilitation for Cocker Spaniels who have become destitute for diverse reasons. Most breeds these days have their Rescue Officers and their telephone numbers are listed by the R.S.P.C.A. kennels and many police stations.

The Cocker Spaniel Club has one official Rescue Officer who is appointed by the committee members and two assistants are also nominated. Mrs Olive Norfolk ('Tarling') founded the scheme at the suggestion of the local R.S.P.C.A. branch several years ago and it expanded steadily under her management. Mrs Wendy Sharp ('Hilgard') is today the main officer keeping a special eye on the northern parts with Mrs E. Portlock ('Carmis') and Mrs G. Foster ('Merriquest') assisting in South Wales/the South-West and southern England respectively. Mrs Sharp is responsible for keeping a record of all dogs handled, where they originate, where they go to and a stated reason as to how the dog appeared in need of help. An assessment must be made of its apparent temperament and notes made on its condition and health.

Dogs are never purchased nor are they sold to new owners; for income the scheme relies solely on help from fund raising activities, donations, legacies and the many Cocker Spaniel people who give generously. When a dog is placed in a new home, the new owner is asked for a donation to the fund, leaving the amount to him or her to decide. Most are glad to subscribe what they can afford; of course, there are always those who 'forget' what would seem to be no less than a moral obligation to further the effects of such good and honorary work.

It is not unusual for more than one hundred animals to be reported annually, and most of these are happily re-housed. It will be realised that the Rescue Officers have often to make difficult decisions: it is becoming increasingly common for some owners to just 'dump' their dogs and, if these are not taken into care as in need of rescue, there always exists the uneasy feeling that they might be turned out of the home eventually and need emergency help. Unfortunately, some individuals constitute a serious problem to the rescue team by virtue of their bad temperament. Dogs which are totally unreliable, either through their early environment or perhaps faulty breeding, may well have to be refused and the only sensible action with potentially vicious and dangerous animals is euthanasia.

All the work of the Rescue Officer and the assistants is quite voluntary. Telephone calls are carefully monitored as are boarding kennel bills and veterinary expenses (when involved) and submitted to the Cocker Spaniel Club Treasurer. The addresses of the ladies mentioned in this section are:

Mrs W. Sharpe
20 Old Broadway
Withington
Manchester M20 9DF
Tel. 061 434 5627

Mrs E. Portlock
Littlemoor Barn
Broad Street Common
Nash, nr. Newport
Gwent
Tel. 0633 283463

Mrs G. Foster
2 Beveridge Lodge
Stelling Minnis
nr. Canterbury
Kent
Tel. 030384 261

7 The Dog Show

Many of the breed's most famous breeders and exhibitors, past and present, are comprised of folk who, when buying their first Cocker Spaniel years ago had not the slightest idea of showing him in competition. People find out later, when the dog has grown on and someone who 'knows' the breed has commented favourably upon his worth as a specimen that they get an urge to put him into competition with others of his kind.

Show bench competition in dogs, although intense in its rivalry, can prove an intensely interesting hobby. Paradoxically, it is sometimes precipitate for a newcomer to be *too* successful in the early stages of his career in the show game. Admittedly, he might have a first class Cocker and one well worthy of his wins, but it is most unlikely that every judge will find the dog a winner, even in company which he has beaten before. A lot of exhibitors are unable to accept easily the occasional defeat that every fancier has to bear at times, especially after having savoured success. For this reason, it is better for them to win by 'easy stages'. Those who win too soon, later to find themselves also-rans, seldom last in the breed and the thin veneer of enthusiasm they have acquired will crack and fall away as they become dejected and disillusioned. It is best to go 'through the mill' in this dog game, most of those who do making good fanciers who set a lasting mark in Cockers.

Preparation

To enter the show game properly takes a lot of time and preparation. If you have been fortunate enough to find yourself with a good dog, or wishing to exhibit, gone out and bought a show dog ready-made, this is only the first step. The second is to bring the animal into show condition, an essential which some people tend to overlook – appearing to think that if the Cocker is good enough in his points this will suffice. They forget that other dogs, equally as good, some even better, will be present at the show and all points being equal it is probably the dog in good coat and condition who will win. This means he must be given properly balanced feeding, adequate exercise and conditioning to bring him into peak form. His mind too must not be overlooked for he must appear alert and eager on the day of the show.

Even when you have him looking the part, he needs still to know what to do when he enters the ring and it may well be that this too could apply to his handler for that matter! The main thing is that the dog should not be upset on the day by show ring bustle and noise, quite apart from the handling which may be meted out to him by the judge. To prepare him for what initially is a bit of an ordeal he should receive firm training in show manners and deportment.

Training for show

Training should commence early, say from five months, when the dog must be induced to stand while on his collar and lead. This will entail taking him to some quiet place, free from distractions, and with a titbit or two as a reward for good progress, gain his confidence and co-operation.

Once the puppy seems ready to work with you, lift him then gently return him to the ground in a 'show' stance which you will want him to assume every time you present him to a judge. This posture requires the forefeet and forelegs to come down straight and parallel from the body, not too wide, not too narrow. They should run in line with the hocks of the hind legs which must be similarly placed. As you position the dog say 'Stand!', steadying him gently as you do so. He will invariably stand still for a moment or two, when he should be praised and rewarded with a titbit. Gradually, he will stand for longer periods until you are able to complete the exercise with the lead lying on the ground. There is always a chance that a dog trained in this way will become too much like a statue, thereby losing much of his personality and expression. The best way to offset this is to keep his attention riveted and eager by holding a titbit in your hand while the dog is standing firm. Of course, if you are lucky enough to have a Cocker who will stand 'four-square' naturally and without manual assistance, then you have no problems. Such a dog's propensity should be encouraged and must be used to your mutual advantage. As soon as the puppy is reasonably well behaved and clearly under your control he should be brought into a busier atmosphere, something more akin to the noise and bustle he is likely to encounter in a typical dog show ring. This could be a public place, but a good idea is to join an Obedience Training Club. Most districts have their own working society and The Kennel Club will be pleased to give you the name and address of the secretary of one in or near to your town. Here your dog's elementary training can be rounded off nicely and he will learn not only to co-operate with you, but to absorb show ring atmosphere and etiquette. Once he is six months old you might prefer to try him out at a small show – one unlikely to affect his career if he disgraces himself! An Exemption show is useful in this respect and such events are referred to in Types of Shows.

Many young dogs resent being handled by a judge, who to them is a stranger. Some judges are a bit rough in the way they handle exhibits and it is not unknown for a youngster, standing nicely at his first show to be toppled off balance by a judge's prod or the heavy pressure of his hand. A dog unintentionally abused in this way may well be spoiled for exhibition for some weeks after the event, needing reassurance to regain his confidence. To offset this, get all your friends and visitors to handle your dog in the way a judge might, i.e. by opening his mouth to inspect the teeth, running hands over his head, skull and body as well as his genitals – all these things as often as possible. The dog will soon become quite resigned to this procedure, and learn to suffer the various indignities with composure.

This type of training when the pupil is young, should be effected at first in short sessions – ten minutes at a time being long enough. The training time can extend to half-an-hour as the dog gets proficient, and longer than this is considered unwise as he will become bored, less co-operative and even resentful of his expected duties.

A dog should not be taken into the ring to compete against others unless he and his coat is in superb bloom. To show him in an ill-conditioned coat would be against his best interests as a show dog and will militate against his marks for general appearance.

Types of shows

There are a variety of shows from which the beginner can take his pick; most of these being advertised in the dog journals *Dog World* and *Our Dogs*, one at least which should be read weekly in order to keep abreast of news and events in dogdom. The Exemption Show provides four classes for pedigree dogs and is often organised in conjunction with a charity appeal or fête. It is not bound by the usual Kennel Club Rules and Regulations although most of the disciplinary rules apply. Unlike other shows, an exhibit need not be registered at The Kennel Club in order to enter and novelty classes such as 'Dog with the nicest eyes' etc. prove popular especially with children exhibitors. Cross-bred dogs too are permitted to attend and compete at Exemption events.

The simplest form of official dog competition is a Match, which is not really a show, rather dog matched against dog, the contestants being eliminated one by one until a final winner emerges. Then there are Sanction and Limited shows run by district canine societies for the benefit of members and to recruit new members; these shows abounding as they are most popular with beginners. They are informal although run strictly according to dog show rules, making good training ground for new dogs as well as tyro owners. The competition provided can be in Cocker Spaniel classes when scheduled as well as in any variety breed classes. From such shows a lot can be learned by watching, listening and participating, quite apart from making a useful introduction to the bigger shows where wins are so coveted. These are the Open and Championship Show events, the latter especially being more important for at such shows challenge certificates can be won and champions made. Open shows like the other foregoing shows mentioned are often unbenched, although many of the big annual events are benched as indeed are all championship shows. Entry fees vary according to the type of show.

Registration

It is important when registering your Cocker that you select a name which is not only attractive but has an impact as a typical breed name. For example 'Merry Monarch' is a good name for a Cocker whereas names such as 'Bill', 'Nell', 'Lassie', while being nice enough as pet names are too commonplace to use as registered names. If you are unable to evolve a suitable name yourself, The Kennel Club will provide one.

When you have decided which show you will attend, ring or write to the show secretary and obtain the show schedule which will come to you with an entry form. The schedule will list the classes, giving a definition for each so that you know under what terms of contract you can enter. For your first show, perhaps two classes will suffice, especially if your dog is still in puppyhood. The Puppy Class will seem an obvious choice, but remember this class allows the entries of puppies between the age of six to twelve months and if your exhibit is a mere six or seven months old he will be giving a lot away to the average eleven monther. However, you may consider the experience and training he will get from the afternoon out will justify being an also-ran. Then there is the Maiden Class, usually for exhibits who have never won a First Prize of £1 or more. This is usually a well-filled class, but you will have the comfort of knowing that the rest of the competitors in it are beginners like your dog or at most non-runners at previous shows.

No dog can be exhibited at a show held under Kennel Club Rules and Regulations unless he is registered. If you have already applied for a registered name and paid the requisite fee (details of all Kennel Club fees will be found in Appendix 2) and the name has not been confirmed by the date for closing entries, you should put the letters N.A.F. (Name Applied For) after the chosen name when you have inscribed it on the Entry Form. Should you have purchased a dog already registered from another person, then this dog must be transferred to your name as the new owner. There is a form and fee for doing this too, but if the transfer has not been confirmed officially by the last day for posting entries, you should put the letters T.A.F. (Transfer Applied For) after the registered name.

Australian C.C.
winner: Miss C.
Jenkins' Stonemill
Orient Express

Make sure that you enter every detail on the Entry Form with care. Many an important prize award has been forfeited due to incorrect details being submitted by a careless owner. Such incidents are very disappointing but they can be avoided with a modicum of care. Watch too the closing date for sending in your entries to the show executive. This rule is very firmly applied and any entry which arrives with a postmark later than the scheduled and advertised date for closing of entries will be rejected.

At the show

On the big day, with your Cocker Spaniel spick and span and in good fettle, try and be at the show venue in good time to allow yourself and the dog time to settle down in the already noisy and unusual atmosphere. Make sure you have all the equipment you need with you. You will need a brush and comb and titbits. If the show is a benched one, provide yourself with a bench-chain, water bowl and food for the dog and yourself. Best take a blanket too to set down in the bench for the exhibit's comfort. However, never feed the dog before he has been into the ring, no matter how late in the day this is. If you relent and do so, you will probably find yourself with a sleepy, indifferent dog on your hands with no desire to show himself or behave as he has been trained to.

Mr H. Jones' Sh. Ch.
Matterhorn Morning
Mist

The average dog will respond to his first show in two ways. Either he will be full of excitement at seeing so many strange and interesting dogs in the confined space of the hall or he will become moody and nervous, wondering what is happening to him. However, with reassurance from his owner he will soon settle down and be ready for his classes.

You will have learned your official ring number either from the show catalogue or from your dog's bench which will have his number on it. Some dog show societies send these on by post prior to the show; others hand them over to exhibitors as they enter hall or the ring to compete, and you should pin it to your person in a conspicuous position. Ring Stewards will arrange you and the other exhibitors in the order required and the judge standing at one end of the ring will call over each exhibitor one by one for their dogs to be judged. When you are called, approach to within a couple of yards from the judge and set up your dog such as you did when training him. Most judges like this done so that they can circle round the dog taking in his visual points. The judge will then make contact with the dog, examining him manually, checking the mouth, head, ears, eyes, ribs – in fact every part of his body. Then, with just another glance round the dog he will wave you to walk away from him. This will allow him to assess the dog's hind action and you should make sure that the dog is moved at a steady jaunty pace, neither pulling forward nor dragging back or he will be penalised accordingly. When you reach the other end of the ring you should turn smartly and your dog should be trained to turn in regimental fashion with you, moving easily and effectively back to the judge who will be watching closely the Cocker's forward gait and balance. Stop a few paces before the judge to see if he has further points to check, but he will probably signal you back to your place in the ring, and proceed to the next exhibit and so on until all the contestants have been judged. This does not mean, however, that you should relax vigil on your own exhibit for one moment. If the judge has taken a liking to your dog he will almost certainly steal an occasional glance at him and if you are allowing your dog to fidget, sprawl, look sleeply or roll about, then he may well fall in the judge's estimation. Keep an eye on neighbouring exhibitors too; some rival exhibitors being capable of little acts of intentional sabotage such as obscuring you from the judge's view or letting their own ill-mannered dog distract yours from his show ring duties.

When the judge has made a complete round of your class he will then wish to place the exhibits in his estimated order of merit. The normal procedure is to draw out first the winner and direct him to the centre of the ring, second, third and reserve placings following in due course. Occasionally, there is provision for V.H.C. (Very Highly Commended) and H.C. (Highly Commended) awards and these too would be selected in that order. However, do not exult if you are the first picked out – it is possible that the judge before finalising his awards will interchange a few of the original positions and you may find yourself not first but third or even lower down the line. This sort of thing is part and parcel of the dog game, making it exciting for all concerned!

At some of the shows you attend you will win, at others, even in similar competition, you will be beaten. It is best to accept that this will happen right from the start of your show career. It is common in dogs and if it did not occur, then that would be an end to dog shows. Everything would be so 'cut and dried' that the same dogs would win and the same dogs lose all the time and no one would bother any more to compete. Dogs vary week by week, even day by day. A good and promising youngster can go plain, become coarse, acquire a limp, lose bloom and a hundred and one other things to set him back. The dog he beat last month, a bit 'raw' at the time has since developed well, is now in fine coat and has acquired a lot more poise and confidence than he had initially. His handler has improved with him and now he beats his earlier rival quite easily.

The main thing is that if you are beaten in the ring – whether fairly and squarely or not – it is best to accept defeat and take it calmly. Nothing will be gained by recriminating the judge and your rivals. People will interpret such scenes as due to petty jealousy and brand you as a poor sport. It is better to chalk any sad affair to experience. If you think the judge has 'robbed' you, then you have the prerogative of deciding whether or not to show under him again. The best way is to give him another chance and then if it seems your doubts are justified leave him alone for good. A good judge like a good dog gets to the top in spite of sundry set-backs. Poor ones might sparkle a bit for a time, according to the strength of their personality, but eventually they find their own low level.

Judges of the breed

The following is a list of U.K. Judges who are approved by the Kennel Club to award Challenge Certificates in the breed up to October 1985.

Alsop, Mr L.
Anderson, Mrs H. B.
Annetts, Miss M.
Armstrong, Mr M.
Arthur, Mrs D.
Arthur, Mr T. H.
Back, Mrs L.
Bailey, Mrs A.
Baldwin, Mrs D.
Baldwin, Mr J. R.
Baldwin, Mrs K.
Barney, Mrs D.
Bebb, Mr R.
Bebb, Mrs T. M.
Becker, Miss P. E.
Bell, Mr H.
Bentley, Mrs P.
Blake, Lt Cdr H.
Borman, Mr T.
Braddon, Mr J. H. J.
Brewer, Mr J.
Broadley, Mrs G.
Brown, Mr J.
Browne, Mrs N. P.
Bryden, Mrs R.
Caddy, Mr G.
Caddy, Mrs J.
Cahill, Mrs D.
Cahill, Mr J.
Cardy, Mr T.
Carey, Mrs J. E.
Casembroot, Mrs J. de
Clarke, Mr D. R.
Clarke, Mr J.
Clibborn, Mrs V.

Cloke, Mrs A. L.
Clover, Mrs J.
Connolly, Mr J. H.
Coulton, Mrs E.
Cox, Mrs E. M.
Crawford-Wallace, Mrs M.
Creamer, Mr T.
Creamer, Mrs K.
Crisp, Mr R. W.
Crowther-Davies, Mrs D.
Cudworth, Mr J. P.
Curran, Mrs F.
Darby, Mrs D.
Darby, Mr E.
Davies, Mr I.
Davies, Mrs J. G.
Dobson, Mrs E.
Donaldson, Mrs M.
Duke, Mr F.
Easton, Mr R.
Fagan, Miss D. M.
Findlay, Mr G.
Flye, Mr R.
Forster, Mr T.
Forward, Mrs M.
Fosbrook, Mr B.
Foss, Mrs V.
France, Mrs M.
Froggatt, Mr E.
Gillespie, Mr J.
Gillespie, Mrs J.
Godall, Mrs J.
Gracey, Mr T. J.
Grayson, Mrs P.
Hahn, Miss D. M.

Hall, Mr A. G.
Hall, Mrs E. L.
Hamilton, Miss F.
Hampton, Mrs O.
Harris, Miss M.
Heavisides, Mr T.
Hillary, Mrs V.
Holmes, Mrs K.
Hubbard, Mr H.
Hussain, Prince
James, Mr R. M.
Jones, Mrs A. M. (MBE)
Jones, Mr H.
Jones, Mrs S. G.
Kane, Mr F.
Keenan, Mr R. T.
Kemsley, Viscountess
Kyle, Mrs A.
Lester, Mrs P.
Lucas-Lucas, Mrs V.
Mace, Mr J.
Mackenzie, Mr D.
Macmillan, Miss J.
Mansfield, Mr A. S.
Maris Bray, Mrs J.
Masters, Mrs P. L.
Matthews, Mrs B.
Matthews, Mr F.
McCormack, Mr L. E.
McEntee, Mrs P. (Dunn)
McFarlane, Mr K.
Moody, Mr A.
Moore, Mr P.
Morgan, Mr D. W.
Neilson, Miss P.
Norfolk, Mr J.
Norfolk, Mrs O.
Owen, Mrs D. E.
Page, Mr D. L.
Parkin, Mr G.
Parkinson, Mr W.
Parsons, Mrs R.
Pascoe, Mr S.
Prince, Mrs W.
Rees, Mr K.

Rennie, Mr J.
Ritchie, Miss B.
Robertson, Mrs E. S. (Retired)
Robertson, Mr W.
Robinson, Miss D.
Robinson, Mrs M.
Roslin-Williams, Mrs M.
Salter, Mr R.
Schofield, Mrs D.
Schofield, Mr P.
Shaw, Mrs P.
Simpson, Mr A. E.
Smith, Mrs J.
Snary, Mrs M.
Spooner, Mrs M.
Stalker, Mr G. E.
Stirling, Miss K.
Stone, Mr J.
Strawson, Mrs B.
Struthers, Miss M.
Sutton, Mrs C.
Sutton, Mrs E. B.
Trench, Mrs D.
Trotman, Mrs P.
Turner, Miss L.
Tyson, Mr J.
Walker, Miss J.
Walmsley, Mr H.
Watkins, Mr D.
Webster, Mrs A.
Webster, Mr A.
Weir, Mr A.
Wilberg, Mr K.
Wilkinson, Mrs M.
Williams, Miss G.
Williams, Mr G. F.
Wise, Mrs P. M.
Wood, Mr G.
Woodhouse, Mr A.
Woolf, Mr P. C.
Woolf, Mrs P.
Worrall, Mr D.
Wright, Mr H. G.
Yates, Mrs V.

Miss B. M. Mingay's
Sh. Chs. Kenavon
Merryleaf Kismet
and Kenavon Joyful

P. and J. Lester's
Sh. Ch. Quettadene
Emblem

Best in Show Winners at the Cocker Spaniel Club Championship Shows since 1946

The coveted title Show Champion (Sh. Ch.) did not exist until 1958. However, dogs who had won three Challenge Certificates under three separate judges prior to 1958 were afterwards allowed the title Show Champion.

1946 *Hyperion of Ware
1947 *Tracey Witch of Ware
1948 Falconers Mark of Ware
1949 Ch. Oxshott Marxedes
1950 Ch. Oxshott Marxedes
1951 Sh. Ch. Tracey Witch of Ware
1952 Sh. Ch. Joywyns Blue Boy of Ware
1953 *Sixshot Sugar Bird
1954 Goldenfields Benito
1955 *Goldenfields Merry Maiden
1956 *Colinwood Silver Lariot
1957 Ch. Colinwood Silver Lariot
1958 *Broomleaf Black Eyed Susan
1959 *Astrawin Aphrodite
1960 Ch. Colinwood Siver Lariot
1961 Mighty Rare of Ware
1962 Sh. Ch. Bouffante of Broomleaf
1963 Sh. Ch. Glencora Black Ace
1964 Sh. Ch. Ronfil Rememberance
1965 *Topbrands Blue Prince
1966 *Colinwood Jackdaw of Lochneill

1967 Sh. Ch. Wells Fargo of Wirdens
1968 Sh. Ch. Lochranza Strollaway
1969 Sh. Ch. Lochranza Strollaway
1970 Sh. Ch. Astrawin Authentic
1971 Sh. Ch. Broomleaf Blithe Spirit
1972 *Bournehouse Starshine
1973 Sh. Ch. Lochranza Newsprint
1974 Sh. Ch. Bournehouse Starshine
1975 *Chrisolin Cambiare of Styvechale
1976 Sh. Ch. Bournehouse Starshine
1977 Sh. Ch. Ramiro of Ronfil
1978 Sh. Ch. Bitcon Silver Model
1979 *Westdyke Weel Ken't Man
1980 *Quettadene Black Jade
1981 *Gemma of Asquanne
1982 *Olanza Pure Magic
1983 Sh. Ch. Bitcon Hot Goss
1984 *Quettadene Emblem
1985 *Matterhorn Misty Morn
1986 Sh. Ch. Canigou Mr Happy

*denotes dogs who later became Show or full Champions

With acknowledgements to Ian Scott, Esq.

8 The Cocker in Sickness and Disease

Although your veterinary surgeon is the right and proper person to consult when your dog is sick or hurt, it is useful to be able to recognise the symptoms of virus and bacterial diseases as well as the more common ailments by which the average dog is often beset. In the following section, which is necessarily brief, first-aid measures are given and these should be administered with care pending arrival of the expert.

Immunisation

Having your dog immunised against the dreaded diseases of Distemper, Hard Pad, Hepatitis and Leptospirosis today constitutes no problem. Every veterinary surgeon is able to perform this service at a nominal fee. The vaccines which have been developed by veterinary science are available according to the personal preference of the user and the country concerned. It is advisable to discuss the matter of immunisation with your own veterinary surgeon and be guided by him. No matter whether your Cocker is valuable or not he has a right to the protection these vaccines can offer. The age at which a puppy should be inoculated will vary according to the proprietary brand of the vaccine; some requiring a youngster to be about two months old for the 'shot' to be effective, whereas others prefer the puppy to be at least twelve weeks of age. With all vaccines it is wise to check whether 'booster' shots are recommended; these being given every one or two years thereby establishing maximum protection. The fact that your dog has been adequately covered against the incidence of disease should not prevent you from exercising every normal precaution for at least ten days following the inoculation. This will allow the antibodies reasonable time to rally against any attack by canine virus or bacteria. Normal antibiotic defence in the Cocker whelp is given by a substance called Colostrum, which exists in the dam's initial milk flow for at least twenty-four hours. This is a globulinous matter which acts as an immuniser against disease for the first few weeks of the whelp's life, its effects tapering away almost up to the point when man-made vaccines are injected for continuity of protection. This is why hand-reared youngsters, i.e. puppies who have never savoured their dam's milk, are usually prone to disease unless their deficiency is corrected by artificial means.

Immunity of about three weeks can be given against the virus diseases of Distemper, Hard Pad and Hepatitis, using appropriate vaccines approved by your veterinary surgeon. The dog owner is well advised to study his Cocker closely, understand his nature, characteristics and pattern of his habits, so that anything unusual in his manner will serve as a warning light to the watcher, preparing him for further signs of sickness. Make sure you know what a dog's normal temperature should be (101.4°F.) – although small puppies sometimes register half a degree more than this. Any temperature over 102.5°F. is one for concern, but if 103°F. and over, then the dog should be isolated immediately and the veterinary surgeon called in. Sub-normal temperatures of say 100°F. require close attendance of the patient pending veterinary diagnosis; this excludes the temperature of 99°F. or less of an in-whelp bitch about to have her puppies.

Keep by you a good quality half-minute blunt end clinical thermometer. To use this correctly first shake down the mercury in the stem to below 97°F. Lightly smear the bulb end with 'Vaseline', then gently insert for one minute into the dog's anus, holding him steady meanwhile so that he does not jerk away or try to sit down, thereby smashing the instrument. The temperature can then be read and the thermometer thoroughly disinfected after use. Make sure that you have a good stock of bandages in various widths, also reliable antiseptic and disinfectant preparations are at hand. The wise dog owner will know too just where he can lay his hands on suitable size splints in case of a broken limb. Cotton wool should be easily available also the common poison antidotes like salt, mustard, washing soda and hydrogen peroxide, items to be found in most households. Information as to how these should be used to make a poisoned dog vomit is well worth acquiring as immediate action in such emergencies can well save a dog's life.

Major Ailments

DISTEMPER

At one time this virus disease was a scourge on dogdom. It usually attacks puppies within their first year, but any age of dog can contract the disease which is very infectious and is capable of wiping out an entire kennel. Although a victim of the disease can recover, there exists an unpleasant aftermath which is liable to affect the dog's nervous system, possibly his brain. This after-effect is known as Chorea, which is like St Vitus' Dance, parts of the body and limbs twitching convulsively and for which there appears no cure or even much relief.

However, this disease is of only moderate consequence today, as it is easily controlled by the many excellent vaccines now produced by veterinary chemists. Distemper causes inner body inflammation, the initial symptoms being loss of appetite, lassitude, some sickness and discharge from the eyes and nostrils. The eyes will become bloodshot and 'gummed up' and should be carefully swabbed over with a mild solution of boric acid, or similar. Food will later be rejected completely and the dog will be in a tucked-up position suggestive of abdominal pain. There will be a dry, hoarse cough and an antipathy to strong light. Odorous, dark-coloured diarrhoea can be expected, also vomiting, the temperature being around 103°F.

The patient should be nursed quietly in a darkened room, cleaning him up at regular intervals and with minimal fuss. Light feeding such as boiled water to which a little honey has been added is ideal and should be continued, gradually increasing to easily digested slightly more solid foods as the patient mends. Ensure that the dog's living quarters (which of course must be completely isolated from the main kennel) are airy yet draught-free.

The best way to prevent the occurrence of this unpleasant disease is to have a puppy inoculated when he is about three months of age. There are a number of different methods of immunisation, all good, as far as is known. 'Booster' doses should follow later in life to maintain immunity, but your veterinary surgeon will advise you on all these matters.

FAMILIAL NEPHROPATHY

At the present time very little can be reported in respect of this very serious condition which is worrying many senior breeders. The Animal Health Trust's Small Animals Centre has contributed with value on the subject under the auspices of Dr D. F. Macdougall, Ph.D., B.V.M.S., M.R.C.V.S., and his colleagues.

Puppies were vaccinated at 10–12 weeks of age, urine samples being collected monthly and at five months all had normal kidney function and blood pressure readings. Monthly blood tests were conducted and arrangements made to collect the first small pieces of kidney tissue (biopsies) under general anaesthesia. Immediately prior to these initial biopsies the new urine test for fibrinogen degradation products gave a positive result for one of the bitches. This was a particularly significant finding as careful examination of the kidney biopsy confirmed the early presence of the disease a full nine months before the bitch showed evidence of kidney failure. This proved the value of the urine test in early diagnosis.

The remaining four puppies were carefully monitored up to the age of 23 months and it was shown that they were free from the disease and likely to remain so. Three were found homes at that stage and as Dr Macdougall points out (*Cocker Spaniel Club Year Book 1983*) although clear of the disease themselves, the results of their regular testing of their urine and related tests gives no indication with regard to their possible 'carrier' status. Thus, they have been placed on the understanding that they are kept as pets and not used for breeding.

The original response to the urine screening programme continues to be disappointing. Up to 31 December 1983 ninety-nine urine samples had been tested and 15 per cent proved positive. Only positive results were continued with, negative results giving no indication with regard to the animal's carrier status as clearly stated on the individual urine sample reports. Dr B. Cattanach became involved with the genetic aspects of this serious condition and his advice was gratefully acknowledged.

For the guidance of new members, the Cocker Spaniel Club recommends the procedure for examination as follows:

1. The owner takes the dog to his own veterinary surgeon and requests the animal to be examined with a view to the issue of a certificate under the scheme.
2. The veterinary surgeon examines the dog and if, in his opinion, it would be worthwhile having the dog examined under the scheme, suggests a referee from the B.V.A. panel.
3. The owner contacts the referee and makes the necessary appointment.
4. The owner presents the dog to the referee together with the Kennel Club registration certificate and any related transfer certificates.
5. The referee examines the dog and signs the report. He then gives one copy to the owner, sends one copy to the B.V.A., another copy to the owner's veterinary surgeon and keeps the fourth copy for his records. The owner should not send his copy of the report form to either the B.V.A. or the Kennel Club as the issue of a certificate will be automatic if the report is favourable.
6. The agreed fee for this certificate and report by the referee is nine pounds at the present time.
7. The B.V.A., on receipt of the report from the referee, issues a certificate if the report is favourable.
   Definitions in Register of Dogs:
   I.C. = Interim Certificate in B.V.A./K.C. Scheme
   P = Permanent Certificate in B.V.A./K.C. Scheme.

HARD PAD

This is actually a more virulent 'cousin' of Distemper, the symptoms being similar, although even less pleasant than that disease. Strictly speaking it is a form of Encephalitis and therefore serious. Following on to the usual symptoms of Distemper, there is a stage when the pads of the feet swell and harden, possibly with similar effects on the facial points and soft parts around the abdomen. The dog will lapse into a fever and may froth at the mouth, finally reaching a stage of spasms and convulsions which usually ends fatally.

Treatment is as for Distemper, but a successful vaccine has been developed and is used in conjunction with the one for Distemper and Hepatitis, the inoculation being given usually in one shot.

HEPATITIS
Correctly known as Canine Virus Hepatitis, also Rhubarth's Disease, this can prove speedily fatal unless dealt with immediately, young stock succumbing easily to the virus. The disease inflames and damages the liver and blood vessels, sometimes bringing on jaundice. It can have the effect of inducing sterility, especially in a bitch. The symptoms are again similar to Distemper, notably loss of appetite with acute thirst, a high temperature of 104°F. and prostration. It is an insidious disease in that a dog might give every sign of having recovered only to collapse a few hours later. It is believed that the virus remains active in some victims months after reported recovery.

A reliable vaccine is available used in conjunction with preventative immunisation against Distemper and Hard Pad.

LEPTOSPIROSIS
Two forms of leptospiral disease are known to veterinary science. Leptospiral Jaundice (*L. ichterrohaemorrhagia*) comes from contact with the urine of rats, attacking the dog's liver, causing jaundice and internal haemorrhage, frequently proving fatal. The other form (*L. canicola*) which passes from an infected dog to other victims, is somewhat lesser in its effect, although the bacteria is believed to damage the kidneys. Dogs affected can be seemingly cured, the vaccines available being very reliable, but often some debilitation of the kidneys has taken place, ill-effects not becoming apparent until later in life, as Nephritis.

Where rats abound it is important to exterminate the pest; all dogs in the kennel (and nearby, if possible) being injected with vaccine as a preventative measure. The possibility of extended kidney damage can be offset at least to some extent with high grade protein feeding such as fresh raw meat, cheese, eggs, etc. The symptoms of an infected dog are similar to those seen in cases of Distemper, together with a high fever which entails the patient's complete isolation from his fellows, treatment being given as advised by the veterinary surgeon. Loss of weight, diarrhoea, intense depression, a strong desire to sleep and some yellowing (jaundice) in the whites of the eyes will be noted. The temperature is usually registered at 104°F. It is not a lengthy sickness and the phase has often passed after a week.

COCCIDIOSIS
This is very infectious and an entire kennel can be quickly affected. The parasite, not unlike the one which attacks fowl, lives in the small

intestines causing severe diarrhoea which is often marked with blood. The dog loses weight very quickly, and seems to lose interest in life. It is important to harden up the motions and the first move to achieve this is to take the dog off all meat, confining him to milky foods. As the disease is spread via the faeces it is essential to maintain absolute cleanliness in the kennel, swabbing down with warm water and disinfectant several times a day. The veterinary surgeon will be able to ease the position and hasten the cure.

PARVOVIRUS ENTERITIS

This tiny virus (its diameter is less than one millionth of an inch) is one which causes apprehension in the dog breeder. It is comparatively new, being unknown before 1978. Similar to feline enteritis its symptom is severe and frequently fatal gastro-enteritis in the dog, affecting usually the puppy just out of weaning stage, although sometimes older dogs are affected. The virus is unusual in that it reaches the intestine by way of the circulatory system instead of passing through the alimentary tract. It would appear that an infected dog could pass on the disease either by contact or by its excretions. Temperatures can be either normal or sub-normal and faeces are frequently blood-stained. Heart failure is often caused by damage to the heart muscle.

Immediate veterinary attention is called for when the disease is suspected. Incubation period is 5+ days, infected animals vomiting followed by diarrhoea. Veterinary treatment will include fluid therapy and antibiotics. There is an excellent vaccine available now with the veterinary world and this will invoke a high level of protection given initially at 15 weeks although some vets recommend it be given first at 6 weeks and again at 15 weeks. It is important to maintain booster doses annually. Dogdom is still watching carefully the progress of this vaccine.

PROGRESSIVE RETINAL ATROPHY (P.R.A.)

This is a congenital disease of the eye and one which is causing much concern in canine circles. It is hereditary and broadly speaking one would say that any animal which suffers from it must have received the genes for such blindness from *both* parents, although neither parent may be actually blind. Thus, the genes for blindness are recessive. If the gene for blindness is carried by one parent only, then the offspring will not be blind, but will be *carriers* of blindness. If, however, both parents carry one gene each for blindness (though not blind themselves) they themselves are carriers: both genes may come together and their offspring may be blind or they may inherit one gene from each and be carriers. But the difficulty is to know which puppies may be carriers and which may be sound. If any question of blindness occurs it is extremely unwise to continue breeding the sire and dam, though the fault probably lies somewhere in the grandparents on either the paternal or maternal side. The symptoms rarely manifest themselves until a dog is mature, so unless one is suitably forewarned it is extremely difficult to weed out the culprits until too late. *The Cocker Spaniel Club Year Book of 1969* published for the first time the register of dogs tested for Progressive Retinal Atrophy. The basis for this was the information collected by Mr G. C. Knight, FRCVS, DVR of London at the Championship Show of the previous year, with additions from private tests and from the B.V.A./K.C. Scheme after this was extended to include Cocker Spaniels. The age limit for our breed for the final certificate is five years, but as many cases of P.R.A. can be diagnosed well before the age limit, members are advised by the Club to take their dogs, particularly breeding stock, at an early stage. If there is no evidence of P.R.A. at this examination, an intermediate certificate will be issued. The final certificate will not be issued until the dog reaches the age of five years. Early examination with an intermediate certificate of as many dogs as possible will obviously help in the control and elimination of the disease.

TETANUS

This is usually known as Lockjaw, and although not common in dogs it should be watched for and if encountered dealt with by an appropriate vaccine which is available. The germ strikes through an open wound, producing a poison capable of striking the nerves and causing acute muscular contraction. The dog will move stiffly and occasionally twitch when standing or at rest. The best treatment is to nurse the dog in a dark room, give light, tasty meals and ask the veterinary surgeon to prescribe a sedative as the animal will almost certainly be suffering from shock.

RABIES

Although virtually unknown in Britain, the 1969 scare which meant the extermination of many wild animals in and around a Surrey town made people aware of its implications. The disease is an ancient one, still common in India and the East, affecting the dog's functional nervous system when the virus is introduced into his blood stream. The bite of a rabid dog therefore is likely to cause rabies or hydrophobia as it is sometimes known, because in course of the disease the victim appears fearful of water, but in fact cannot drink because of paralysis in the throat. An acute change in the dog's normal behaviour pattern can be expected, and he will usually become snappy, even vicious. This propensity increases with dropping of the lower jaw and progressive paralysis of the hind limbs especially. The dog will wander away from home and this is when the real danger starts for he may bite and infect other animals, wild or domestic, who in turn can bite others who become secret carriers of the virus. Humans are equally prone to the disease which eventually works its way to the brain, resulting in death. Several countries, notably Great Britain employ a system of quarantine to guard against rabies. This, although considered severe by some has proved its efficacy on innumerable occasions.

There is no announced cure for the disease as yet, but useful veterinary vaccines are now available which will immunise your dog against this unpleasant and powerful virus.

Minor ailments and physical conditions

ABNORMAL BIRTH
When a puppy arrives head first at the opening of the womb this is normal birth. When the hind feet are presented first, it is known as a breech birth and offers no complication as a rule. Puppies presented sideways or in twisted form will probably need veterinary assistance, according to the seriousness of the situation.

ABNORMALITIES
These usually entail congenital deformities, viz. Cleft Palate, Hare Lip, the two conditions often appearing together. The normally flat roof of the mouth is cleft, making it impossible for the puppy to suckle its dam as no vacuum can be formed in the mouth. The milk will bubble out through the whelp's nose and it will not thrive, dying within a day or so. It should be humanely destroyed at once.

ABORTION
A bitch will abort her puppies, usually due to a knock or blow, or even infection in the uterus. If abortion occurs early in the gestation period, the dam will sometimes dispose them herself without the owner's knowledge. This is sometimes unwittingly taken as a 'miss' and a free stud service claimed! Symptoms when noted in a bitch in whelp are extreme fatigue, sickness and haemorrhage at the vulva.

ABSCESS
A hard, painful swelling filled with pus, such as a boil. It can be caused by localised grime and is more likely to affect a dog temporarily out of condition. Raise the swelling to a head with fomentations, then squeeze away the poison matter. Dress carefully after swabbing with mild antiseptic.

ACCIDENT
In case of internal damage and to offset shock condition, keep the dog quiet in a warm, dark room. Re-assure him with words and caresses until arrival of the veterinary surgeon.

ACNE

This is seen in pus-filled pimples which eventually break forming scabs. The rash is found usually on the under-belly and is very irritating. Witch hazel dressing and medicinal powder will normally deal effectively with the condition, but it is wise to get veterinary opinion.

ANAL GLANDS

There are two small glands beneath your Cocker's tail, one on either side of the anus. An inheritance from the wild state they are no longer used, but this does not prevent them getting clogged with waste matter. This causes inflammation and irritation, the dog rubs his rear along the ground and seems in some pain. The trouble can be eased by squeezing the glands to expel the offending substance. This operation should be attended to regularly as there is always a danger that abscesses might form.

APPETITE

Lack of: In small puppies this is usually a sign of worms, which must be expelled allowing the youngster to revert to normal feeding. In older dogs it could indicate a soreness in the mouth, causing the dog pain when eating. Examine teeth and gums and soft part of underlip. Always take the dog's temperature in case he is sickening for something as this is an initial symptom of the virus diseases.

Perverted: It is not uncommon to find dogs, especially puppies and bitches eating coke, coal, stones, even their own excrement and that of other dogs. Again, this may be due to worms, but usual cause is some chemical deficiency in the bloodstream which can be corrected either by change of diet (with an emphasis on raw meat) or vitamin additives.

Abnormal: A bitch in whelp will usually increase her food intake. It is a common symptom just prior to her oestrum. The phase frequently reverts back to normal, but the owner should regulate meal quantities meanwhile.

ASTHMA

A complaint which usually affects older dogs, especially those carrying too much weight. Breathlessness and wheezing respiration are to be expected, sometimes accompanied by a dry cough. If allowed to persist the heart can be affected. However, change of diet to include mainly fresh raw meat is necessary, also gradual stepping up of daily exercise in order to reduce the dog's weight. The veterinary surgeon should be informed so that he can prescribe professionally.

ARTIFICIAL RESPIRATION

The whelping dam uses this system to induce breath into her new born puppies. She prods, pushes and tumbles them with her tongue until they 'squeal' into life. A puppy which does not respond can be resurrected by giving it the 'kiss of life' and a dog almost drowned can be brought to life by laying it on its side and depressing the ribs with the flat palm of the hand. Release at once, and repeat the pressure alternately every two seconds.

BALANITIS
A discharge from the penis, probably commoner in a dog not used at stud than one in regular service. A mild solution of antiseptic (dilution of 1:5 in tepid water) should be syringed beneath the sheath at regular intervals until the condition is relieved.

BITES
Providing the dog can reach the affected area and lick it clean, this will prove the speediest cure. However, if he finds the bite or cut is in an inaccessible place, wash the immediate region and treat with good antiseptic solution. If cuts are deep and open, drip in iodine or antiseptic first, then bandage and prevent dog from relieving himself of the dressing by using the conventional Elizabethan collar which your veterinary surgeon will describe.

BLADDER
Inflammation of: The best aid to relief is to flush out the system with plenty of water, but it is not easy to get a dog to drink more than he wishes at one time. Usual cause of this condition is Cystitis and it is therefore advisable to get veterinary advice. If stones are the cause, then it will be necessary to employ surgery to remove them. Incontinence, i.e. inability to hold the water in the bladder, is usually found in bitches heavily in whelp or in old dogs. When an in-whelp bitch is so affected she may be worried at her lapses and need an owner's patience and understanding, for this is no more than a phase after which she will quickly return to her usual house-cleanliness. In an old dog it could indicate kidney trouble in which case your veterinary surgeon should be asked to examine the dog and prescribe.

BLINDNESS
A puppy is born blind and seldom opens his eyes until the ninth or tenth day of his life. Congenital blindness on the other hand is a serious matter; progressive retinal atrophy (night-blindness, etc.) being a major problem today in dogdom. This becomes a case for the expert and such advice should be sought without delay. An animal so affected must not be considered for any breeding programme.

BREASTS
Congestion of: Frequently, when a bitch's milk is not taken up quickly enough by her puppies encrustment will ensue around the teats.

Inflammation occurs and the bitch becomes distressed, biting at herself and sometimes inducing abscesses. Her fluid intake should be reduced at once and the teats bathed around to reduce and dispose of the 'caking'. The bitch should then be milked by hand and if your veterinary surgeon can prescribe to ease her discomfort this should be arranged.

BREATH
Bad: Not uncommon in a Cocker Spaniel of advanced years, caused by tartar in the teeth and ulceration in the lip folds. Constipation and sundry infections can also induce bad breath. All areas likely to be responsible should be swabbed with a mild solution of antiseptic and the dog's teeth scaled and cleaned.

BREATHING
Laboured: Found usually in an out-of-condition dog, especially noted after exercise. It may suggest anaemia or a heart condition in which case the veterinary surgeon should be asked to examine the patient.

BRONCHITIS
Often contracted after a soaking or bad cold. Dogs allowed to sleep in a draught will sometimes become bronchial, coughing, wheezing and with a high temperature of about 103.5°F. It is important to bed them down in warm airy atmosphere, giving light, tasty meals. In bad cases the Bronchitis Kennel will have to be employed, the patient being forced to breathe in vapour of Friars' Balsam or similar medication.

BURNS
Always treat for shock as well as the localised damage. The dog should be kept quiet in warm, darkened room and reassured by his owner. A teaspoonful of bicarbonate of soda and warm milk with glucose added should be administered. Burn-ointment should be stored ready for such an emergency, but failing this first-aid measures will include sponging with strong, newly made tea. This applies only to mild burns and scalds. Higher degree cases should be referred at once to your veterinary surgeon.

For convalescence build up the patient with high protein diet, especially raw meat.

CANKER
Ear canker is by no means uncommon in Cocker Spaniels and is a condition usually affecting the inner ear canal. There is inflammation and discharge of a brown substance which is waxy and unpleasant in its smell. This needs careful cleaning away from the ear and this is best effected by wrapping a tight small wad of cotton wool round the blunted

end of an orange stick and teasing out the wax – an operation which needs to be done very gently. There are a number of medications such as drops and powders on the market to deal with canker and one or more of these can be employed or your veterinary surgeon will deal with the condition. Sometimes due to the intense discomfort canker will cause it may prove necessary to give the dog a mild sedative before he beds down for the night.

CATARACTS

The lens of the eyes will become covered with a milky film in advanced cases, the sight being seriously affected. The condition is often found in older dogs, but cataracts can be inherited and young Cockers with such a legacy from their ancestors can seldom be treated satisfactorily even with expert surgery.

COLIC

Stomach pains brought on by the dog eating something which does not agree with him. The symptoms include a tucked-up position which indicate severe stomach pain. The best domestic medicine if colic is diagnosed is a small teaspoonful of bicarbonate of soda in warm milk. Following this, the patient should be kept quiet in a warm room.

CHOKING

This has to be treated as an emergency, for it is probably caused by some foreign object lodged in the dog's throat. To remove it, two people should be employed, one to prise open and hold steady the dog's jaws, the other to hook out with his index finger the offending object. Should this prove impossible then to actually push it down the dog's throat might prove the best alternative. To offset the possibility of such accidents, take care to keep all lethal objects like tiny rubber balls, knobbly small bones and children's toys out of a dog's reach. Cut up his meat into safe chunks too; a greedy dog can easily choke on a piece of unmanageable size, although often enough he manages to vomit it up to safety.

COLLAPSE

Only a serious malady is likely to cause complete collapse in a dog, although often it can be occasioned by shock, following a fight or an accident. Animals so affected may well have a weak heart, but in any case always treat for shock, raising the dog's hindquarters above head level with the patient laid on his right side. If he is *conscious* two drops of brandy on the back of the tongue will help, otherwise give nothing orally. All cases of collapse call for veterinary attention.

COLITIS
Inflammation of the colon, diarrhoea and loss of weight being normal symptoms. As in humans it is not a very satisfactory condition to treat, but in the initial stages milky and careful diet of a nutritious nature with nursing in a warm room will have good effect.

CONCUSSION
A heavy blow on the head will cause this and the dog should be put in a dark room at once and the veterinary surgeon called. Ice packs can be applied to his head and he should be well bolstered around with stone hot water bottles covered with blankets.

CONJUNCTIVITIS
Inflammation of the eyelids around inner edge, causing watering and soreness. Although likely to recur, the condition can be relieved with a simple veterinary ointment or 'Golden Eye Ointment'.

CONSTIPATION
This is due usually to too much biscuit meal with insufficient vegetable oil matter. The dog's motions should be watched carefully and wrong feeding will often be revealed. There are many good canine laxatives available, but medicinal paraffin or similar oil will be found effective. A daily teaspoonful will normally act mildly and effectively until the matter is resolved. Ensure however, that no unnatural cause exists such as a blockage in the bowel and any prolonged difficulty in evacuation should receive medical attention. A dog once cured should receive a tonic and be toned up with plenty of daily exercise.

CYSTS
The commonest form of cyst is interdigital, that which appears between the dog's toes. He will be in some pain and attempt to lick the swellings, either making them worse or bringing them to a head so that they eventually burst. Failing the latter, each foot should be put in warm water or hot fomentations applied and a mild antiseptic solution applied to the wound once the pus has been dispersed. Final dressing should be with medicated powder. Cysts sometimes appear on the body and these can be dealt with in similar fashion or by surgery. However, before treating locally in any way it is advisable to experiment with the dog's diet. A complete change of feeding, i.e. from raw fresh meat to a good proprietary brand or vice versa has been known to dispose of cysts within two weeks. If the remedy lies in such a method it is preferable to any other.

CYSTITIS
(See Bladder Inflammation).

DIABETES

The two main symptoms are thirst and hunger. The coat becomes dry and staring and general condition is poor. Lassitude, vomiting and diarrhoea. A sprinkle of bicarbonate of soda should be included with every meal, which should be mainly of raw meat, once the motions have been made firmer. Diabetes is normally a condition for the veterinary surgeon to treat.

DIARRHOEA

This is a symptom of many disorders as well as the virus diseases, already mentioned. It is the body's way of disposing its toxic substances which have upset the digestive system. Diarrhoea should be a warning to an owner to seek its cause, making sure whether it is merely a simple case of worms or part of the pattern of serious infection. If the condition continues for two days the veterinary surgeon must be consulted without further delay. Feeding should be confined to warm bread and milk which will help to bind the motions and make them firm; no raw meat should be allowed until diagnosis has been made. All motions should be kept away from other dogs in case of infection.

DISCHARGES

Any form of discharge is usually indicative of infection and it is wise to call in your veterinary surgeon to ascertain the cause. Mucus discharge from the nose suggests virus disease, ear discharge a form of canker and vaginal discharge, while being common enough in bitches soon after whelping is a debilitating condition capable of developing into peritonitis if not halted. Any unusual discharge should be suspect and dealt with summarily. Penis discharge (Balanitis) has been referred to already and discharges from the mouth suggest bad teeth or ulceration in the folds of skin on the lips.

DISCHISIATIS

In effect a double row of eyelashes turning in slightly from the lids and brushing the eyeballs, causing the dog great discomfort. Surgery would appear the best way of dealing with this matter, for extraction of the lashes with tweezers from time to time does little more than relieve the situation.

ENTROPION

This is a hereditary condition of the eye, either the upper or lower eyelids, sometimes both, turn inwards. Surgery has been employed successfully, but the condition is more common in breeds which have bred for a smaller eye than normal.

EPISTAXIS
Nose-bleed. Ice packs on the organ will usually alleviate, even stop the flow quickly. The common cause is a blow on the nose, but if the bleeding persists the matter should be referred to the veterinary surgeon who will examine the dog for foreign bodies in the nostrils.

EPULIS
This is a hard fibrous growth in the gums, sometimes to be found in veteran dogs. If necessary, it can be removed by surgery, but if the dog does not appear inconvenienced it is better left alone.

EPILEPSY
Fits of short duration are not uncommon in small puppies during the course of teething. The youngster's eyes will glaze over, he will froth a little at the mouth possibly, then keel over. In such instances keep the dog quiet in a warm room until he recovers. More serious fits which are occasioned during the aftermath of a virus disease or due to an accident or some hereditary condition are seldom entirely curable.

GASTRO-ENTERITIS
Diarrhoea, sometimes flecked with blood is a common symptom, this becoming darker and more bloodstained if allowed to remain untreated, when it can result in death. Stomach pain, vomiting (which is often white and frothy) and loss of weight will be noted and the dog should be put on a very light diet of milky foods, warm bread and milk being particularly good. Raw meat should be withdrawn entirely while the dog is loose in his motions.

HEAT-STROKE
A dog left unattended in the hot sun or penned in the back of a closed vehicle will sometimes collapse from heat stroke. A dog so thoughtlessly treated should be allowed a limited drink of cold water to which a little salt has been added; then bathe the animal gently all over his body with cool water, letting him rest for an hour or two in a well ventilated room.

HERNIA
There are several kinds of hernia conditions. The one usually encountered is the *Umbilical* form which is a bump on the navel. It is often caused by the dam biting roughly at the umbilical cord when she whelps her puppy. Few veterinary surgeons would consider a small example of this form of hernia an unsoundness and although these protruberances look a little unsightly when the dog is in puppyhood, they are ofen quite insignificant when the animal becomes mature. If it is thought necessary to remove one, a veterinary surgeon can do this quite easily while the dog

is in his first year. Home methods which include strapping back the bump for several weeks seldom prove effective and serve only to irritate the dog. Other forms of hernia include the *Inguinal* kind, more often experienced by a bitch than a dog. This is seen in a swelling behind the inguinal teats which are situated in the groin. This hernia condition, and also the *Scrotal*, *Diaphragmatic* and *Perineal* hernias, the last-named sometimes found in the veteran dog, are more serious forms and require professional attention as soon as detected.

HIP DYSPLASIA

This is a genetic problem involving the degeneration of the *acetabulum* (hip socket) into which the femoral head (knuckle bone) should easily ride. The disease is one of great antiquity, in humans at least, and may well have affected dogs for centuries too. Some experts disclaim it as a congenital disease as it does not appear to be present in the dog at birth, although there is little doubt that it is actually hereditary. However, what is not apparent at birth may well be extant and this feature of the condition has to be considered.

As stated, it is a ball-and-socket problem and a good deal of friction and erosion is engendered in the joint as the animal grows into maturity. As these stresses continue, lameness gets progressively worse.

It cannot be diagnosed without the support of correct analytical scrutiny of an X-ray plate by a competent authority trained to acknowledged high standards. The B.V.A. (British Veterinary Association) manages a joint scheme with the Kennel Club, known as the Joint B.V.A./K.C. Hip Dysplasia Scheme and this lays down certain rules for procedure by veterinary surgeons. Details are available from the Kennel Club and these come with an application card for submission of the dog's particulars with radiograph for scrutiny. The scrutineers have a panel which sits monthly and they either pass the dog as being free from H.D. when a qualifying certificate is issued, or the dog is failed, whereupon a letter is sent to this effect. For borderline cases a 'breeder's letter' is sent to the veterinary surgeon to pass on to the subject's owner.

Fortunately, H.D. affects Cocker Spaniels very little. The disease is commoner in the longer-boned breeds, but this does not mean that a vigilant watch should not be kept for signs of it in individual animals. It is not possible to state categorically that a dog has H.D. without the support of a competent analytical survey. If a dog is being examined in the show ring and he stumbles at the turn around or hops at every other step, swings his haunches unduly when going away or evinces odd characteristics in his gait then H.D. might be suspected, although patella luxation (kneecap dislocation) may be contributory to such peculiarities of gait. Another pointer may be a dog's reluctance to rise from a seated position, but guesswork is not always conclusive and the situation must be confirmed. It can even be possible that a dog moving well may be dysplasic, as instances have occurred that radiographic examination of the hips has revealed H.D. in a form which does not cause lameness! Even so, only an X-ray plate which has been scrutinised professionally will reveal the truth.

It must be remembered that H.D. is a complex hereditary condition which must never be ignored or allowed to penetrate our breed as it has done others. Breeders must ensure that they avoid at all costs individuals who are its victims.

INDIGESTION

This can be caused by eating unsuitable food or eating too much. Stomach pain will be experienced, also bowel noises. Treatment is to give the dog a little stomach powder mixed in warm milk and to stop feeding him for a day or more according to his response. When feeding re-starts ensure that he has sensibly balanced meals in modest quantity.

LICE

Most dogs at some time or other in their lives receive these unwelcome visitors. They cause intense irritation and their eggs, often to be seen attached to the coat should be picked off and burnt, otherwise they will hatch out in about five days. The best way to deal with them in the first instance is manually; pick out as many as you can, using a metal comb, finger and thumb. Then bathe the dog in a suitable anti-parasite preparation of which there is a good selection on the market. Let it dry on the coat, then brush off, completing process with electric dryer and/or towel. There are also some good dusting powders available which will deal effectively with these parasites and these should be used according to the makers' instructions.

MANGE

A common enemy of the dog, this appears in various forms, as wet and dry eczema, 'dermatitis' and parasitic mange. Unless pernicious most of these can be dealt with satisfactorily and cleared up nicely, although the time taken doing this can vary from days to months according to the severity of the attack.

Follicular Mange: This is a common form and at one time a killer mange, being very difficult to cure. Even litters became infected and had to be put down. However, thanks now to modern veterinary medicine the mites are reasonably easy to eradicate. Breeds such as the Cocker Spaniel are less prone to it than some of the short-coated varieties but any signs of bareness around the eyes, hocks and other thin-coat areas should be a warning signal. The parasites burrow into and live in the hair follicles and the patches made usually start off about half-inch in diameter, gradually spreading over the body and becoming reddish-brown in hue, changing in final stages to a grey, mousy shade. Occasionally, pustular spots form and when erupting emit an unpleasant smell. There are a number of proprietary ointments etc. available, but the wise breeder takes advantage of the latest veterinary preparations to be had. Ensure too that the patient is well exercised and kept in good health. Often a change of diet will expedite a cure.

Sarcoptic Mange: This is a form of dry eczema and is similar to scabies which humans experience. It often affects dogs who are out of condition, thus emphasising the necessity for an immediate toning-up course coupled with nutritive feeding. The initial rashes are frequently on the soft skin of the belly and groins, resembling acne. The skin becomes harsh and dry, the dog's coat begins to stare, then spots appear as the hair falls out. It may prove necessary to try a variety of medicines and ointments to find a cure, but this is a good policy to adopt with all skin complaints as they seem to vary in effect and intensity from dog to dog. It will be found that the average dog's digestive powers are adversely affected and it is important to guard against the patient's general debilitation. The popular ointment among dog breeders confronted with mange of this kind is one made from a base of flowers of sulphur. This is readily obtainable as are lotions for bathing the dog.

Ringworm: This is an unpleasant form as it can be contracted by humans. The patches resemble rings, hence the name. This is a fungoid disease and should be treated at once, there being remedies available to effect a speedy cure. It need hardly be warned that children should be kept away from dogs with ringworm.

POISONING
Give the victim an emetic immediately, useful forms being available in any domestic household. A dessertspoonful of common salt in a quarter pint of water or a similar solution of mustard being particularly effective. A small knob of common soda will work well too. Call in the veterinary surgeon immediately and try and track down the source of the poisoning so that he can instruct you in the particular first-aid required. Keep the patient quiet and warm and soothed as far as possible.

ROUNDWORM
Few dogs escape infestation from the common roundworm. It usually becomes necessary to dispose of worms in young puppies and this is today a simple job which can be done without the old system of starving the subject first. There are many veterinary preparations available, all of them good, or your veterinary surgeon will attend to the matter for you. Unless this is done, an infested puppy will never thrive and may become an easy victim for any canine disease which besets him. It is common

practice to treat a bitch for possible worms before breeding with her. The process can do no harm even assuming she is free from them at the time, and it may save heavy infestation in her young. Care should be taken to regularly disinfect puppies' quarters, coupled with frequent washing down of the premises. This will ensure the kennel is not contaminated. When the worms are emitted they will come through either the puppy's mouth or its anus. Vermicelli-like in their appearance and usually in a tight skein they should be shovelled up and burnt at once. It is best to wait until the puppy is at least five weeks old before worming him – certainly the process should not take place until weaning has been commenced and six weeks of age is a good time to do it. However, if the youngster is so bloated with worms as to necessitate worming at say four weeks or younger then a veterinary surgeon should be asked to act in the matter.

RUPTURE
(See Hernia.)

STINGS
Wasps and bees are the main offenders and their stings can be serious, although an isolated sting can be easily dealt with as a rule. Dogs are liable to snap at and trap these insects in their mouths, so in and around the mouth is the usual place for stings to occur. The foot is another commonly affected place, especially in late summer when wasps are lethargic and are pawed at. Dab on at once a strong solution of antiseptic or bathe round the sting (after extracting the barb) with strong bicarbonate of soda and water mixture (2 tablespoonsful well stirred into a pint of water). If the sting is on the foot, stand the member in a shallow bowl of the same solution or rub the sting with a lump of common washing soda.

TAPEWORM
An unpleasant parasite which is said to be passed on by the flea and/or by eating rabbit. As its name suggests it is like a length of narrow creamy coloured tape composed of segments which on their own look like fat grains of rice. The presence of a tapeworm can sometimes be revealed by one or more of these segments adhering to the dog's anal region or in his stool. Care should be taken to ensure that other dogs in the kennel do not come into contact with infected stools and the kennel area should be systematically swabbed down with disinfectant twice daily. The victim will become depressed, lose weight and evince no interest for food, as a rule, although the opposite symptom is encountered at times. The worm can easily be expelled with modern veterinary drugs. Often they are found to be many feet in length and a dog so cleared of this pest will immediately pick up in health and begin to thrive.

WEIGHT

Loss of: This can be due to a variety of causes, the commonest being insufficient feeding. However, the dog should be examined for existence of virus or bacteria diseases, anaemia, kidney disorder, gastro-enteritis (with accompanying diarrhoea), bovine tuberculosis, diabetes, growth or even worms.

Administering medicines

LIQUIDS

Keep the dog's mouth closed, but open up the pocket formed by the lower lip where it joins the corner of the mouth. Pour the medicine into this opening either from the bottle or spoon. Do not hold the head right back, but only slightly forward. Usually the liquid will go straight down the dog's throat, but if he seems to be holding it in his mouth, close the lips and raising his head slightly, rub the throat. This will cause him to swallow and imbibe the lot.

TABLETS AND POWDERS

The dog's mouth should be opened, one hand already holding the pill, which should be placed quickly as far back on his tongue as possible. Then close the mouth, rub the dog's throat and the pill will disappear. With powders, these should be put into a 'scoop' made of the wrapping paper and tipped on to the dog's tongue, a similar procedure being adopted.

9 Glossary of Terms and Points

Beginners especially are sometimes confused by the host of descriptive and semi-technical words they encounter in dogs. These are more evident perhaps, in dog show critiques and fanciers' discussion meetings. The parlance is quite extensive, many of the words used being more appropriate to specific breeds, the word 'Harlequin' for example (not included in this Glossary) being virtually confined to Great Danes as a coat marking description, whereas 'hard-mouthed' and 'gun-shy' are terms which apply to the retrieving and field breeds, such as our Cocker Spaniel, when applicable. Some terms are in general use throughout dogdom, and the picturesque 'cow-hocks', 'in-toed' and 'camel back' indicate faults in most known breeds.

Here is a diagram showing the Points of the Cocker Spaniel. It can be used in reference to various terms contained in the Glossary.

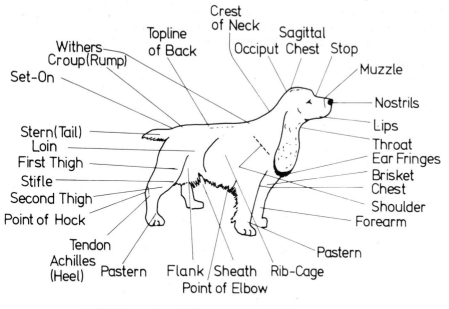

POINTS OF THE COCKER SPANIEL

FIG. 4. POINTS OF THE COCKER SPANIEL

AFFIX: A name granted by The Kennel Club General Committee to a breeder registering or changing the name of a dog. Where the Grantee of a registered Affix wishes to use it when naming a dog bred by him or which was bred from parents which were bred by him, then the Affix must be used as a prefix (as the first word of a dog's name). Otherwise it must be used as a suffix (the last word of a dog's name).

ANGULATION: A term used to describe relationship or the angle made by bones when forming joints, generally directed to haunch-bone, tibia and femur in the hindlimbs and shoulder bone, radius and humerus in the forelimbs. Poor angulation suggests obtuse, therefore weak formation; good angulation infers satisfactory coordination of the bones.

ANORCHID: A male dog without testicles, and unable to procreate. Can be confused with cryptochidism, although it is a rare condition.

APPLE HEAD: Rounded (like an apple) on top of the skull. Seen in the Toy Spaniel, but undesirable in many breeds.

APRON: Frill or ruff of long hair lying below neck in long coated breeds.

A.V. (A.O.V.): Any Variety/Any Other Variety: A show term found in Definition of Classes indicating that different varieties or breeds are eligible for competition.

BACK-CROSSING: To breed a cross-bred dog or bitch back to one of its parents or to a dog of the same breed as one of its parents.

BAD-DOER: A dog who does not thrive in spite of good care and attention. Such dogs are seldom good feeders and are fastidious even from puppyhood.

BALANCE: When seen in profile, from the front also the rear, the dog's outline should be pleasing, without exaggeration and evenly conformed as required by the breed Standard. The picture should be maintained to give stylish and sound action when moved both ways.

BARREL: Referring to the ribs, the cage of which should be well sprung and rounded, akin in some ways to a barrel. The term is used rather to emphasise the necessity for ample lung room.

B.B./B.O.B.: An abbreviation for Best of Breed.

BEEFY: Coarseness, especially in the region of the hindquarters.

BELTON: Blue and white and orange and white flecked coats seen in some gundogs.

BITCHY: Disparaging term applied to a male dog with feminine lines and expression.

BITE: Refers to relative position of upper and lower incisors of the forward jaw when closed. See: OVERSHOT, UNDERSHOT, WRY MOUTH, etc.

BLAZE: A white bold marking running from forehead to nose. Sometimes used erroneously to describe a white collar.

BLOCKY: Stocky, either in head or body.

BLOOM: Physical well-being evinced by glossy coat.

BONE: A dog with ample bone is one normally well-endowed structurally, the limbs especially having the feel of strength and spring. A dog with poor bone may lack calcium, one with too much bone evince coarseness.

B.R.: Blue Roan: A coat marked almost equally in blue and white.

BRACE: Two dogs of the same breed or two exhibited together in the Brace Class.

BREEDER: (or Br: abbreviation): The legal owner of a bitch at the time she whelps.

BRISKET: The part of the dog's body in front of the chest and between the forelegs.

BROKEN COLOUR: When a coat is mainly of one or self-colour, but is broken up by white or other colour markings.

BROOD BITCH: A bitch kept solely for breeding use. Such an animal should be strong, typical and sound both temperamentally and physically.

B.S./B.I.S.: Best in Show.

BURR: Folded formation of inner ear.

BUTTERFLY NOSE: When the nostrils show flesh coloured patches with the black pigment.

CAMEL BACK: Another name for Roach Back.

CAT FOOT: A compact, round foot which is well arched as in the cat.

C.C.: Challenge Certificate. A Cocker needs to win three Challenge Certificates, each under a different judge at a different championship show held under Kennel Club Rules and Regulations to become a Show Champion. This applies to shows in Great Britain.

C.D.: Companion Dog. A title gained by a dog who has passed a test in Obedience. C.D.X. = Companion Dog (Excellent). A superior award in Obedience work.

CH./CHAMPION: See: Challenge Certificate.

CHEEKY: Abnormal fullness of the cheek muscles.

CHEST: The arched, upper section of the neck.

CHINA EYE: A blue eye or wall eye.

CHOPS: Pendulous lips.

CLODDY: Thick-set build.

CLOSE-COUPLED: Well put together and short from last rib-bone to haunch-bone.

COBBY: Compact and close-coupled.

COLLAR: White marking around neck on an otherwise dark coat.

CONDITION: Refers to health, physical and temperamental, coat and general bloom.

CONFORMATION: The form, outline, structural perfection and physical features of the breed according to its Standard.

CORKY: Lively, perky and active with good type.

COUPLINGS: See: Well-coupled.

COUPLE: Two of a breed. Refers usually to Hounds.

COW-HOCKED: When the points of hocks turn in towards each other, thereby turning out the rear feet. A fault.

CROUP: The region which abounds the sacrum down to set-on of the tail.

CROWN: Highest part of the skull.

CRYPTORCHID: A male dog whose testicles have not descended in the scrotum. A dog in this state will be unable to procreate, neither can he compete in exhibition under Kennel Club Rules.

DAM: The mother of puppies, the term being used from the time she whelps them.

DEW-CLAWS: A fifth claw with little or no purpose to be found on the inside of front legs and sometimes found on hind limbs. These should be removed a few days after birth by the veterinary surgeon.

DEWLAP: The loose skin below the throat.

DOCKING: Amputation of a dog's tail to within specified joints, usually done within a few days after birth (see section on subject).

DOGGY: Disparaging term applied to a bitch with male lines and expression.

DOME: Refers to rounded skull of the Spaniel and some other breeds.

DOWN IN PASTERN: Sagging or weakness in the lowest part of legs between knee (or hock) and foot.

DUAL CHAMPION: A dog who has qualified for not only Show Champion status, but qualified for a Working Certificate in the Field.

ELBOW: Joint at the top of the forearm. The elbows should be close to the body and the points of elbow should never turn out. When they do, this is referred to as 'out at elbow' and is a fault.

ENTIRETY: A dog is said to be entire when both the testicles are descended in the scrotum.

EXPRESSION: An outlook, typical of the breed, composed of and formed by size, colour, positioning of the eyes coupled with the use of the ears.

FEATHER: The fringe of hair which adorns the backs of a Spaniel's legs. The term can include fringing on ears and tail.

FIELD TRIAL: Competition in the field, the dogs being judged on their aptitude with game.

FLECKED: When the coat is lightly flecked with another colour, as opposed to a coat which is dappled, roaned or spotted.

FLEWS: The pendulous inner corners of the lips.

FRILL: Hair under the neck and on chest.

FURNISHED: Mature, developed in full.

GAIT: Mode of action, style of movement.

GENES: Units of inheritance, emanating from both parents.

GESTATION: The period of time from conception to birth of the puppies, usually nine weeks or sixty-three days.

GOOD-DOER: A dog who thrives well naturally, always seeming to be in good bloom and eating well.

GOOSE-RUMP: A croup which slopes down too abruptly, the tail seemingly set on too low.

GUNDOG: A dog trained to game in conjunction with the gun.

GUN-SHY: A dog who fears the gun and its report.

HANDLER: A person who handles a dog whether in Exhibition, Obedience or Working duties.

HARD-MOUTHED: A gundog who retrieves game and damages it in the process due to tight grip.

HARE FEET: Feet which are rather long and narrow, the digits splayed as in the hare.

HAUNCH: Region immediately above hip joint.

HAW: Excessive drop or hang of the inner lid of the eye, usually showing bloodshot.

H.C.: Highly Commended. Sixth award placing in exhibition, but normally with no cash value.

HEAT: Season, Period or Oestrum. When the bitch is menstruating.

HOCKS: Equivalent to the ankle in humans. The joints between the pasterns and stifle in hind legs.

HUCKLE BONES: The top of the hip joints.

HUMERUS: The arm-bone. This articulates with lower end of shoulder blade, being slightly curved and lying obliquely to join with radius and ulna to form the elbow joint.

IN-BREEDING: The planned mating of close relatives such as father to daughter, etc. in order to 'fix' certain desirable points, already existing in the mating pair and their background.

INTERNATIONAL CHAMPION/INT. CH.: A dog who has gained the title of champion in more than one country. Officially, this title is not recognised by the English Kennel Club.

LEATHER: The skin of the ear-flap. Widely used to include the ear itself.

LEGGY: Too tall on the leg as to make the dog unbalanced.

LEVEL JAWS: When the upper incisors rest over and upon the lower incisors with no apparent space between them. This is the correct mouth formation in the Cocker Spaniel.

LIGHT EYE: Eyes which are amber or light in colour.

LINE-BREEDING: The planned mating of a dog or bitch with his or her relatives from strains which are similar although not too close. It is common to mate dogs with the same sire and different dams and vice versa, but it is essential that the mating pair are good specimens and closely resemble each other.

LIPPY: Abnormal development of the lips causing them to overhang.

LITTER: Term given to the family of puppies born to the bitch at one time.

LITTER CLASSES: Classes arranged at some dog shows for litters which are not older than three months or younger than six weeks on the show date.

LIVER: A reddish-brown colour, the colour of butcher's offal.

LOADED AT SHOULDER: When the shoulder muscles are over-developed giving an impression of heaviness.

LOIN: Region on either side of vertebral column between last ribs and hindquarters.

LONG CAST: Opposite to short-coupled, similar to long-coupled, i.e. long in back and couplings, particularly with reference to the distance between last rib and hip joint.

LOW SET: Refers usually to a tail which is set on low, but can refer to a dog rather short in the leg, or ears which are set on low to the head.

LUMBER: Overweight in flesh and timber making the dog ungainly.

MAIDEN: A bitch which has not had puppies. In show classification a class open to exhibits which have never won a first prize.

MANTLE: Refers to the darker part of the coat on shoulders, sides and back.

MATCH: Competition conducted under Kennel Club Rules and Regulations between pairs of dogs of the same or different breeds, a system of elimination being used until final winner is found.

MATRON: Refers to a brood bitch.

MERLE: Blue-grey mixture colour of the coat seen in some working breeds. It is usually flecked with black.

MISSING: When a bitch fails to conceive in spite of the fact that the mating was satisfactory and that both animals in the union were normal.

MONORCHID: A male dog with only one testicle descended in the scrotum.

MUZZLE: That part of the headpiece which comprises the foreface, including jaw, nose and lips. Could also refer to a contraption of straps or wire used to stop a dog biting.

N.A.F.: Name Applied For. Indicates that the dog's owner has applied to The Kennel Club to register his dog with a given name.

N.F.C.: Not For Competition. A show term indicating that the exhibit is at the show for display and not for competition.

NOVICE: A beginner in the dog game. In show classification a class open to exhibits who have not won three or more first prizes.

OCCIPUT: The bone at the top of the back of the skull. Although prominent in some Hounds and the old type of Field Spaniel it should not be too evident in modern Spaniel varieties.

OESTRUM: The bitch's menstrual period, sometimes referred to as the 'season', 'heat' or 'showing colour'.

OPEN SHOW: A show held under Kennel Club Rules and Regulations and open to all breeds with no challenge certificates on offer.

OUT AT ELBOW: When the points of elbow turn out and away from the wall of chest. A fault.

OUT AT SHOULDER: When shoulders protrude outwards and loosely, giving an impression of width when viewed from the front. A fault.

OUT-BREEDING or OUT-CROSSING: The mating of entirely unrelated dogs.

OVERHANG: Term given to heaviness or protrusion of the brow.

OVERSHOT: When the upper incisors project thereby making a space between them and the lower incisors. Sometimes known as 'pig-jaw'.

PADS: The cushioned soles of the feet.

PARTI-COLOUR: A coat which is made up by patches of two or more colours.

PASTERN: That part of the leg below the knee on the forelimbs and below hock in the hindlimbs.

PEDIGREE: The dog's 'family tree' showing his sire and dam and the names of his ancestry usually taken back to three or four generations.

PIEBALD: Pied. When a dog's coat is made up of mainly white with large black patches.

PIGEON-CHESTED: When the sternum or breastbone projects abnormally.

PIGEON-TOED: Sometimes referred to as In-toed. When the toes turn in or point towards each other. A cow-hocked dog is often pigeon-toed as is one who is out at elbow.

PIG-EYED: Eyes which are small and close-lidded.

PIG-JAW: See: OVERSHOT.

PILE: Dense or thick undercoat of a long-coated dog.

POINTS: Can refer to the anatomical points detailed by the breed Standard or to nails, lips, eye-rims, nose.

PRICK-EARS: Ears which are carried erect as in a Bull Terrier, French Bulldog, etc.

PUPPY: In law, a dog up to the age of six months, but The Kennel Club treat him as a puppy up to one year of age.

QUALITY: Refinement with Type.

QUARTERS: The fore-parts (forequarters) and hind-parts (hindquarters). The term is usually applied to the latter.

RACY: A dog who although quite well developed is inclined to length and reach which makes him fast in movement.

RANGY: A long-bodied, rather leggy specimen, lacking depth.

RAT-TAIL: A well-rooted tail tapering to a tip and covered with short hair, like a rat's.

RESERVE: The fourth place in show awards, usually without monetary value.

ROACH BACK: When the spine arches upwards from the withers towards the loin.

ROAN: Mixture of coloured and white coat, e.g. blue roan, lemon roan, etc.

RUFF: Long hair standing out from the neck.

RUNNING ON: A doggy term which refers to keeping a promising puppy for several months to ascertain his ultimate worth as a show prospect.

SANCTION SHOW: A show held under Kennel Club Rules and Regulations and confined to members of a canine society, and subjected to special sanction.

SCAPULA: The shoulder blade.

SEASON: See: OESTRUM.

SECOND TEETH: The permanent teeth which replace the first mouth or puppy teeth.

SECOND THIGH: The part of the hind leg which extends from stifle to the hock.

SELF-COLOUR: One colour coat. Sometimes referred to as self-marked.

SEPTUM: The vertical dividing line between the nostrils.

SERVICE: Term used in mating when the dog 'covers' the bitch, i.e. the act of copulation.

SET-ON: Usually refers to where the tail joins the body.

SHELLY: Term used to describe a shallow, ill-developed body.

SHORT-COUPLED: Short in back and loins.

SICKLE-HOCKS: Hocks which are well bent and nicely let down.

SICKLE-TAIL: A tail which is formed like a sickle and carried out and up.

SILENT HEAT: When evidence of oestrum is unseen, i.e. no coloured discharge, in spite of the bitch being ready for mating. Probably due to a hormone deficiency.

SIRE: The male parent.

SLAB-SIDED: Flat-ribbed.

SNIPY: Refers to a muzzle which is pointed and weak.

SOFT MOUTH: A gundog with a soft mouth is one who can retrieve game without damaging it.

SOUNDNESS: A dog is said to be sound when he is in good health physically and mentally and is normal throughout.

SPAYED: A bitch is said to be spayed when her ovaries have been removed surgically, so that she becomes incapable of having puppies.

SPREAD: The distance between the forelegs, i.e. width of front.

SPRING: Refers to the elasticity of the rib cage.

STANCE: Posture.

STANDARD: The official description or word picture of the perfect Cocker Spaniel, drawn up originally by a panel of breed experts and approved by The Kennel Club.

STERN: Tail of a sporting dog.

STILTED: Refers to mincing gait, usually due to upright shoulder emplacement.

STOP: Depression between and in front of the eyes, similar to bridge of the nose in humans.

STRAIGHT IN HOCK: A hock which is almost vertical, lacking bend.

STRAIN: A family or clan of dogs with a distinct bloodline which has stemmed from notable dogs in the past.

STUD: A stud dog or where stud dogs are kept. A dog kept and used for servicing bitches whose owners will pay a nominal fee for his use.

SUBSTANCE: Good substance suggests ample bone and physical development.

SWAY BACK: A dip behind the shoulders at the withers, showing poor muscular development.

T.A.F.: Transfer Applied For. The letters to be put after a dog's name on the show entry form when a new owner has not by that date received official notice of transfer of ownership to his name.

TEAM: Three or more dogs of one breed or variety.

THROATINESS: With surplus and loose skin under the throat.

TICKING: Small flecks of dark hair on a white coat.

TIE: When the mating pair become 'tied' tail to tail while copulation takes place.

TIMBER: Substance and bone.

TOPLINE: The line of the back when the dog is viewed in profile.

TRICOLOUR: Three colour coats, usually white with black-and-tan.

TUCKED-UP: Term applied to posture of dog when his stomach muscles are contracted, either when in pain or naturally according to his breed if say, a dog of the chase, such as Greyhound, Whippet, Borzoi.

TYPE: The qualities characteristic of an individual breed to make him a model of his variety.

TYRO: Beginner or Novice.

UMBILICAL CORD: The cord joining the unborn puppy to the placenta.

UNDERSHOT: When the lower incisors project beyond the upper incisors when the mouth is closed.

UNSOUND: A dog which is unfit either physically, mentally or both. Unsoundness can be inherited or acquired temporarily (such as a broken leg). Anything which causes the dog to fail in function such as in movement, working aptitude etc. can be termed an unsoundness.

UPRIGHT SHOULDER: When the shoulder blade and upper arm joint makes an obtuse angle, causing stilted action.

UPSWEEP: Seen in an undershot specimen when lower jaw sweeps up and out.

VENT: The anal region, sometimes used in reference to the anus.

VETERAN CLASS: A class at dog shows usually for exhibits of seven years and over.

V.H.C.: Very Highly Commended. An award at dog shows fifth in order of merit.

WALL EYE: A term which encompasses the china blue and pearl eye colours, associated with a merle coat.

WEAVING: A form of movement when the dog crosses his front legs one over the other.

WEEDY: Lacking substance and bone.

WELL-LET-DOWN: Refers to hocks which are short and which make good angulation at the joint.

WELL SPRUNG: Refers to ribs which are nicely rounded and elastic.

WHEEL-BACK: A back which is arched from withers over the loins to the hips.

WHELPS: Puppies are termed thus from birth until they open their eyes about ten days later.

WHOLE COLOUR: Self or one coloured coat.

WITHERS: The top of the shoulder blades at the base of the neck.

WORKING CERTIFICATE: A certificate awarded at Field Trials to gundogs who have qualified in working trials and general breed duties. A Show Champion receiving such an award is entitled to the title of Dual Champion.

WRINKLE: Loose skin or folds of skin on foreface and brow.

WRY MOUTH: When the incisors of top jaw cross at one point the incisors of the lower jaw. The worst form of mouth formation incapable of making a clean bite.

Appendix 1

Cocker Spaniel breed clubs and their secretaries

THE COCKER SPANIEL CLUB (THE PARENT CLUB) (1902): Mr A. E. Simpson, Coltrim, Upper Pendock, Nr Malvern, Worcs. WR13 6JW. Tel: (068 481) 360

The following Clubs are associated with the Parent Club in accepting the same standards and ideals. The date is the year of registration of the home Clubs.

THE BLACK COCKER SPANIEL SOCIETY (1968): Mrs D. M. Porter, Tanglewood, 21 Orchard Road, Old Windsor. Tel: Windsor (075 35) 60274

CHESHIRE COCKER SPANIEL CLUB (1936): Mrs A. Rathbone, 4 Harper Avenue, Newcastle-under-Lyme, Staffs. Tel: Newcastle (0782) 624090

COCKER CLUB OF SCOTLAND (1933): Mr and Mrs A. Crichton, 148 Glasgow Road, Garrowhill, Glasgow G69 6EU. Tel: Glasgow (041) 771 2691

COCKER SPANIEL CLUB OF LANCASHIRE (1950): Mrs D. M. Schofield, Cobbles, Norcott Brook, Warrington, Cheshire WA4 4DX. Tel: Norcott Brook (092 573) 353

COVENTRY COCKER SPANIEL CLUB (1951): Mrs M. Allard, 49 Angela Avenue, Potters Green, Coventry. Tel: Coventry (0203) 616893

THE DEVON AND CORNWALL COCKER SPANIEL CLUB (1982): Michael Owens, 299 Fort Austin Avenue, Crownhill, Plymouth. Tel: Plymouth (0752) 775830

EAST ANGLIAN COCKER SPANIEL SOCIETY (1965): Mrs O. Norfolk, Tarling, West Hanningfield, Chelmsford, Essex CM2 8UU. Tel: Chelmsford (0245) 400428

EAST OF SCOTLAND COCKER SPANIEL CLUB (1937): Mrs E. Johnson, Knocktower, Newbridge, Midlothian. Tel: Edinburgh (031) 333 1313

HOME COUNTIES COCKER CLUB (1947): Mrs F. Harness, 24 Tamworth Road, Hertford, Herts. SG13 7DN. Tel: Hertford (0992) 59153

LONDON COCKER SPANIEL SOCIETY (1932): Mr R. W. Crisp, 84 Wembley Hill Road, Middlesex HA9 8EA. Tel: London (01) 902 5726

MIDLAND COCKER SPANIEL CLUB (1923): Mr R. Pain, 'Branflic', 57 New Inns Lane, Rubery, Birmingham B45 9TS. Tel: Birmingham (021) 453 3215

NORTH MIDLANDS AND EASTERN COUNTIES COCKER SPANIEL CLUB (1948): Mrs Prince, Church Farm, Findern, Derbys.

NORTH OF ENGLAND COCKER SPANIEL ASSOCIATION (1942): Mr K. B. Taylor, Broom Cottage, Castle Road, Mop Cop, Stoke-on-Trent ST7 3PH. Tel: Stoke-on-Trent (0782) 515060

NORTH OF IRELAND COCKER SPANIEL CLUB: Mr T. J. Gracey, BEM, 67 Knockvale Park, Belfast BT5 64J. Tel: Belfast (0232) 651394

NORTH WALES COCKER SPANIEL CLUB (1930): Mr D. Gorse, 10A Thornside Walk, Gateacre, Liverpool L25 5PJ. Tel: Liverpool (051) 428 8903

PARTI-COLOUR COCKER SPANIEL CLUB (1971): Mr A. Browne, 26 Grosvenor Road, Shipley, W. Yorks. Tel: Bradford (0274) 592555

RED AND GOLDEN COCKER SPANIEL CLUB (1928): Mrs V. Hillary, 2 Nursery Lane, Hookwood, Horley, Surrey. Tel: Horley (029 34) 4032

ROTHERHAM AND DISTRICT COCKER SPANIEL CLUB: Mrs A. Richardson, 65 High Street, Bolton on Dearne, Rotherham, S. Yorks. Tel: Rotherham (0709) 893425

SOUTH WALES AND MONMOUTHSHIRE COCKER CLUB: Mrs E. Jones, 2 Springfield Close, Cefnpennar Road, Cwmbach, Aberdare, Mid Glamorgan. Tel: Aberdare (0685) 872387

ULSTER COCKER SPANIEL CLUB: Mr T. J. Cardy, Mount Keepe, Glen Road, Lower Castlereagh, Belfast 5. Tel: Belfast (0232) 791267

WEST OF ENGLAND COCKER SPANIEL CLUB: Mr K. Price, 'Bienvenu', Parkend Road, Coalway, Coleford, Glos. Tel: Dean (0594) 3372

YORKSHIRE COCKER SPANIEL CLUB: Mr D. Shields, The Red House, Kirbymisperton, Malton, N. Yorks., YO17 0XL. Tel: Malton (0653) 86 355

Clubs in Eire

COCKER SPANIEL CLUB OF IRELAND: Mrs K. Creamer, 24 Coolgariff Road, Beaumont, Dublin 9, Eire. Tel: Dublin (0001) 371 825

BLACK RED OR GOLDEN COCKER CLUB OF IRELAND: Mrs P. Murphy, 'Auburndale', Grange, Magenby, Carlow, Eire

DUBLIN COCKER SPANIEL CLUB: Mr W. M. McEntee, Dalkeith, Kilteel Road, Kill, Naas, Co. Kildare, Eire

Clubs abroad

ENGLISH COCKER SPANIEL CLUB OF AMERICA INC.: Mrs Kate Romanski, P.O. Box 223, Sunderland, Minnesota 01375

It will be seen that clubs for the Cocker Spaniel's welfare abound in every region. The secretaries listed will be pleased to send details of membership with facilities offered to all enquirers. A stamped addressed envelope will be appreciated. Kindly note that secretaries sometimes change from year to year as this office is usually an honorary one. Should you have difficulty in making contact with the person you want, a letter forwarded to the Secretary, The Kennel Club, 1 Clarges Street, Piccadilly, London W1Y 8AB, will always be transmitted to the correct destination.

Appendix 2

Registrations and Kennel Club Fees

The Kennel Club's headquarters is at: 1 Clarges Street, Piccadilly, London, W1Y 8AB. General Enquiries: 01–493 6651; Registration Enquiries: 01–493 2001; Telegraphic Address: 'Staghound London W1'. Its patron is Her Majesty Queen Elizabeth II with HRH Prince Michael of Kent FIMI its President. The Club's chairman is Mr J. A. MacDougall, M.Chir, FRCS, FRCSE and Senior Executive and Secretary Mr M. H. Sinnatt, CB.

The objects of the club are to exist mainly for the purpose of promoting the improvement of dogs, Dog Shows, Field Trials, Working Trials and Obedience Tests and its objects include the classification of breeds, the registration of pedigrees, transfers etc., the licensing of shows, the framing and enforcing of Kennel Club Rules, the awarding of Challenge, Champion and other Certificates, the registration of Associations, Clubs and Societies and the publication of an annual Stud Book and a monthly Kennel Gazette.

Every breeder should make sure his home-bred stock is registered at The Kennel Club and also insist that his colleague breeders do the same. By so doing, the breed's 'official' numerical strength is increased, and championship show managements will maintain, even improve their support.

Cocker Spaniels prove by their registration figures at The Kennel Club that in Britain the variety is the most popular of the Spaniel family. This may be due to the dog's 'useful' small-to-medium size, always an asset when striving for the popularity stakes, coupled with an easy adaptability to domestic life. In the field, even the veriest tyro can provide his owners with a pleasant afternoon and with the added armament of a lovable and sympathetic nature, a high degree of intelligence and absolute loyalty to his master, it is small wonder the Cocker is in great demand. The breed is an old one with centuries of evolution to boast about. If a breed can get near to perfection the Cocker can. The big Championship shows, Cruft's especially, has popularised Cockers, notably with the breed's Best-in-Show wins. This publicity, not forgetting what the variety has contributed by its natural beauty and charm and usefulness, has proved of immeasurable worth to Cocker Spaniels. Today, it is an established breed known and appreciated in tens of thousands of homes, strongly competitive in the show ring and reproducing itself true to type and quality.

The following are annual (January to December) registration total figures from 1949:

1949	1950	1951	1952	1953	1954	1955	1956	1957	1958
19942	16226	12871	9854	8129	7356	7275	7071	6484	6515

1959	1960	1961	1962	1963	1964	1965	1966	1967	1968
6943	6374	6758	6559	6514	6263	6259	5229	5625	5944

1969	1970	1971	1972	1973	1974	1975	1976	1977	1978
6465	7121	6825	8255	8193	8254	7210	3336	2256	6310

1979	1980	1981	1982	1983	1984	1985	1986 (to June)
9415	9891	8009	7697	8064	7573	7619	3437

The Kennel Club registration figures for American Cocker Spaniels commenced in 1969. They are:

1969	1970	1971	1972	1973	1974	1975	1976	1977
166	309	352	409	530	596	488	285	254

1978	1979	1980	1981	1982	1983	1984	1985	1986 (to June)
369	482	543	459	462	409	405	481	182

Kennel Club Fees (inclusive of VAT at 15 per cent)

Registration Fees, as from 1 October 1985:

LITTER RECORDING/REGISTRATION BY BREEDER
(The total number of puppies in the litter must be declared)   £
Litter Recording Fee (payable in every case)   (each) 5.00
Plus per puppy in litter registered (named)   (each) 5.00
Plus per puppy in litter not registered (unnamed)   (each) 1.00
e.g. A litter of five puppies of which two are registered (named) and three are unnamed will cost £5.00 plus £10.00 plus £3.00
Total £18.00

DOG NAMING BY OWNER:
Registration (Salmon Form 2)   5.00
Registration in Obedience Register (Buff Form 1A)   5.00
Change of Name. Affix Holders only (Pink Form 8)   5.00

	£
TRANSFERS:	
Transfer by new owner	5.00
PEDIGREES:	
Export Pedigree	20.00
Pedigree (3-generations)	3.00
AFFIXES:	
Registration of an Affix	35.00
Affix Maintenance Fee (Annual)	10.00

CLUB FEES: (inclusive of VAT at 15 per cent)

Registration of Title	50.00
Registration of Title (Branch)	10.00
Maintenance of Title	15.00
Maintenance of Title (Branch)	6.00

SHOW FEES: (Effective for all Shows held from 1 January 1986)

General Championship Show – offering more than 20 sets of Challenge Certificates, with or without Obedience Championship	500.00
General Championship Show – offering 20 sets of Challenge Certificates or less with or without Obedience Championship	125.00
Group Championship Show	125.00
Breed Championship Show	30.00
Championship Obedience Show – as a separate event or as part of a Championship Show	30.00
Open Show	20.00
Open Obedience Show – as a separate event or as part of an Open Show	20.00
Limited or Sanction Show	5.00
Primary Show, Match, Agility Test or Exemption Show	5.00
The following Extra Fees as payable for Championship and Open Shows: For each dog entered, over one thousand	.10

Litter recording and registration

The Club records about 70,000 litters and registers 170,000 individual dogs each year and this is the principal service provided for dog breeders and owners. In order to minimise delays and inconvenience in the recording and registration process, it is important that the procedure is fully understood.

A litter can only be recorded if both the sire and the dam are already registered with the Kennel Club. The breeder (owner of the dam at the time of whelping) should submit the application form. The confirmation of mating section on the application form must be signed by the owner(s) of the stud dog at the time of mating. Both the dam and sire must be registered to the persons shown as the owners on the application form.

At the same time as the litter is recorded, individual puppies may be named and registered and, in these cases, individual registration certificates are issued to the breeder who should then give the certificates to any new owner to enable them to record the transfer. If the puppies are not individually named and registered when the litter is recorded, registration forms will be sent to the breeder and these should be given to any new owners and may be submitted to the Club to register individual dogs. It is recommended that individual puppies should be registered at the time of the litter recording to avoid unnecessary delays and inconvenience. Special regulations exist for the registration of imported dogs registered with overseas Kennel Clubs and dogs registered with other recognised Clubs. Information on these special categories can be supplied by the Kennel Club.

Naming of dogs

The Kennel Club endeavours to lay down certain guide-lines to be followed for the naming of dogs in order to minimise the risk of confusion. Consequently, some applicants are disappointed because they cannot give their dogs the names they consider to be the most suitable or appropriate. The following are the main guide-lines in naming dogs which are to be registered:—

(a) Proposed names must not exceed 24 letters including an affix, if any (see next section regarding affixes).
(b) Names of notable persons, countries, and cities should be avoided. Numerals (in figures or in words) and common single word names are not acceptable. Applicants should not use single letters as part of a name or initials or their own surnames.
(c) A name already used to register a dog may not be used again to register another dog of the same breed until ten years have elapsed since the last registration. However, if that name has been entered in the Kennel Club Stud Book, it cannot be used again as the registered name of a dog of the same breed.
(d) Unless representing the affix of the owner, words which have already been used within the dog's pedigree may not be used again as they may constitute an affix held by another person. (In which case the proposed name will not be acceptable.)
(e) Words which have already been used in naming either parent or other puppies within the litter should not be repeated unless application has been made for the word to be registered as an affix.

(f) Always give a second choice of name in order to avoid unnecessary delays and, in the event that both choices are unavailable, the Kennel Club will provide a name which is as near as possible to the applicant's choice, unless the applicant instructs otherwise.

(g) Once a dog has been named, the name cannot be changed except for the addition of an affix.

Affixes

The General Committee may grant an application to register an affix (kennel name) so as to give the grantee, during the continuance of the grant, sole right to use such an affix as part of a name when registering or changing the name of a dog. No application will be considered unless the applicant has bred a dog which has:—

(a) Qualified for entry in the Kennel Club Stud Book, or

(b) Won a first, second or third prize in a Postgraduate, Minor Limit, Mid Limit, Limit or Open Class for the breed at a Championship Show in the U.K.

Where the grantee of an affix wishes to utilise it when registering or changing the name of a dog, it must be used as a prefix, that is to say, as the first word in a name, if the dog was bred by him or was bred from parents each of which was bred by him. Otherwise the affix must be used as a suffix, that is to say, the last word in the name.

An affix consists of one word only, not exceeding 12 letters and must not be hyphenated. The word should preferably be a made up word but may be the name of a house, landed property or village belonging to or connected with the applicant. A word listed in a dictionary is unlikely to be granted as a registered affix. The word cannot be used for the registration of dogs until it has been officially granted by the Committee, but applications for the registration of dogs may be lodged at the time of application for the affix and will be held pending the decision of the Committee. However, this could take up to three months as all applications are published in the Kennel Gazette to give other interested parties an opportunity of lodging an objection.

It is important when using an affix that the ownership of the affix is exactly the same as the ownership of the dogs being registered, i.e. if the affix is held jointly, then registration of the dog must be in the same ownership. It is possible to have a variety of interests in the same affix.

There are two charges for using an affix, consisting of a setting-up fee and an annual maintenance charge thereafter.

It is emphasised that it is not necessary to have an affix in order to register a dog with the Kennel Club, but it is the only way in which a single word can be repeated in naming a litter and, thereafter, that word or affix is reserved for the exclusive use of the affix holder, as long as the annual maintenance fee is paid. In the event of annual maintenance not being paid, the exclusive right to use the word as an affix is withdrawn.

Finally the exclusiveness of the affix is related only to the word itself in its original spelling and does not extend to derivatives or words of similar spelling or pronunciation.

Shows

The Show Department deals with all matters relevant to registered Societies and Shows. There are approximately 1700 Societies registered with the Kennel Club; the register is divided into four categories:—

1. General Canine Societies — Specific areas of the country and for more than one breed of dog.
2. Breed Societies — Specific breed of dog.
3. Dog Training Clubs — Obedience and/or Working Trials.
4. Field Trial Societies — Field Trials.

General and Breed Societies may hold both Breed and Obedience competitions but Dog Training Clubs are restricted to Obedience competitions or Working Trials. Each year over 7000 competitions are licensed by the Kennel Club; these range from very large General Championship Shows at which the Kennel Club's Challenge Certificates are on offer, to Exemption Dog Shows which are licensed to charitable organisations to raise funds.

Events licensed by the Kennel Club:—

Championship Shows — Open to all, Kennel Club Challenge Certificates on offer in most breeds.

Open Shows — Open to all, no restriction on classes.

Limited Shows — Limited to members of the organising Society or to exhibitors living in a specific area.

Sanction Shows — Limited to members of the organising Society with limited level of competition.

Primary Shows — Only members of the organising Society eligible for entry. The number and type of classes are restricted.

Matches — Knock-out competitions held within or between Societies. Only members of participating Societies eligible for entry.

Exemption Shows — Small 'fun' dog shows, licensed to charitable organisations. Kennel Club Registered Societies may not hold such events.

Awards

The Awards Department is responsible for recording the results obtained in competition in Shows, Trials and Tests held under Kennel Club Licence. The results in the higher levels of the above competitions are then collated to produce the Kennel Club Stud Book. Entry is obtained by success in competition only and applies to both dogs and bitches.

On receipt of the marked catalogue the Stud Book qualifying awards, as listed below, are noted and the owners will be allocated a Stud Book Number on initial qualification. Owners are advised automatically and application is not required. The current qualifications for entry in the Stud Book are:—

(a) Dogs winning Challenge Certificates, Reserve Challenge Certificates, or First, Second or Third Prizes in Open or Limit Classes, where Kennel Club Challenge Certificates are competed for in the U.K. when such classes are not subject to any limitation as to weight, colour or other description.

(b) All winners of Prizes, Reserves, Awards of Honour, Diplomas of Merit or Certificates of Merit at Field Trials held under Kennel Club Field Trial Rules and Regulations.

(c) Winners of Prizes or Qualifying Certificates in TD or PD Stakes at Championship Working Trials held under Kennel Club Working Trial Rules and Regulations.

(d) Winners of First, Second or Third Prizes in Championship Class 'C' at Championship Obedience Classes.

Various certificates are awarded by the Kennel Club for the principal winners in Championship competition only.

SHOWS: Challenge Certificates (C.C.) are awarded by the judge of the breed to the best of sex and a Reserve Challenge Certificate (R.C.C.) to the Reserve best of sex in each sex. The judge must be clearly of the opinion that the exhibit to which he has awarded the C.C. is worthy of the title of Champion and that the exhibit to which he has awarded the R.C.C. is in his opinion worthy of being awarded the C.C. should the C.C. winner be disqualified.

Similar certificates are awarded for Obedience Tests, Field and Working Trials.

CHAMPIONSHIP: In general terms the title of Champion or Show Champion is awarded to any Show Dog which obtains three C.C.'s under three different judges provided one of the C.C.'s was obtained when it was over 12 months of age.

As with certificates, the titles of Field Trial, Working Trial and Obedience Champion have differing qualifications but are all based on acquiring a specific number of certificates.

Application is not required for the above certificates which are normally issued some weeks after the Show. However, there are two further certificates for which application must be made:—

1. Junior Warrant	Points are awarded for first places in classes at Open and Championship Shows obtained whilst the dog or bitch was aged between six and eighteen months on the first day of the Show. Application forms giving qualifying details are available on request.
2. Breeder's Diploma	Is available (on request by letter) to the breeders of any form of Champion. The breeder does not have to be the owner.

Kennel gazette

The Kennel Club publishes an official monthly magazine under the title Kennel Gazette and this is available on annual subscription from the Publication Department.

Breed Records Supplement

This is a quarterly publication produced by the Kennel Club in which all registrations, transfers, changes of name, export pedigrees, Champion Certificates, Challenge Certificates and allocation of Stud Book numbers are listed under individual breed sections. When a dog is registered, the last three characters in the registration number indicate in which volume of the Breed Records Supplement the details are recorded. Individual copies of the Supplement are available from the Club, or it is available by subscription.

Export pedigrees

Before a dog can be registered with a Kennel Club in another country, it is necessary to obtain an export pedigree from the Kennel Club. It should be noted that at the same time as application is made for the export pedigree, an application to register or transfer the dog must be completed where the dog is not already registered in the first overseas consignees ownership.

Three Generation Pedigree service

The Club provides a service whereby a Three Generation Pedigree is produced by computer. The aim is to provide dog owners and breeders with a quality pedigree service at low cost. This service is available as an optional extra at the time of registration or transfer or on request for a modest fee.

Obedience and working trials register

Dogs which do not qualify for registration in the breed records, may still be registered in the Obedience and Working Trials register so that they are eligible to enter Obedience and Working Trials held under Kennel Club rules. This register is therefore also open to crossbred dogs and other dogs where the parents are not already registered with the Kennel Club in the breed records. The Club also has special arrangements for dogs registered in the International Sheepdog Society, and the Greyhound Stud Book. For further details of these arrangements, please contact the Kennel Club.

Cruft's Dog Show

The Kennel Club is responsible for the presentation of the Cruft's Dog Show which takes place in February each year at Earls Court. In addition to breed judging, Cruft's includes Obedience Championships, Inter-Regional Competitions and an Agility Competition.

A dog is eligible for entry in breed classes at Cruft's if it has qualified in any of the following ways under the Rules and Regulations of the Kennel Club.

1. If it is a Champion, Show Champion, Field Trial Champion, Working Trial Champion or Obedience Champion.
2. If it has been awarded a Challenge Certificate or Reserve Challenge Certificate at a Show during the year prior to Cruft's.
3. If it has won first prize in certain breed classes at a Championship Show where Challenge Certificates were on offer during the qualifying year.
4. If it has won first prize in certain classes at Cruft's Show in the previous year.
5. If it has been awarded a 5 point or higher Green Star under I.K.C. Rules during the qualifying period.

Membership

All the services listed above are provided by the Kennel Club as the body accepted as controlling authority for Pedigree dogs and for Obedience and Working dogs. It is also a private Members Club with a restricted membership, which does not follow automatically from the use of these services.

Associate Membership, however, is more generally available to people of good standing and repute in the dog world and full details of the benefits of Associate Membership are available on request.

The Kennel Club Junior Organisation has been set up to encourage young people between the ages of 8 and 18 to be interested in the care and training of dogs and to enjoy all kinds of activities connected with dogs.

For further information and appropriate application forms write to: The Secretary, The Kennel Club, 1 Clarges Street, Piccadilly, London, W1Y 8AB. Tel: 01-493 6651.

Appendix 3

A Selected Bibliography

ANON.: *Biography of a Spaniel*, London, 1816.

ASH, E. C.: *The Cocker Spaniel*, London, 1935.

BARROWS, W. and PHILLIPS, J. M.: *The Color in Cocker Spaniels*, Journ. Hered. Vol. 6, 1915.

BASNETT BROUGHALL, N. S.: *The Cocker Spaniel Handbook*, London, 1951.

BISHOP, G.: *Spaniels*, n.d.

BREARLEY, J. M.: *The Book of the Cocker Spaniel*, New Jersey, 1975.

CARLTON, H. W.: *Spaniels: Their Breaking for Sport and Field Trials*, London, 1915 *et. seq.*

COCKER SPANIEL CLUB, The: *Year Books*.

COWPER, W.: *The Dog and the Water Lily*, London, 1798.

DALY, M.: *The Cocker Spaniel*, London, n.d.

DE CASEMBROOT, J.: *The Merry Cocker*, London, 1966.

DOXFORD, K.: *The Cocker Spaniel*, Its Care and Training, London, n.d.

FRANKLIN, E.: *Practical Dog Breeding and Genetics*, London, 1969.

GALSWORTHY, J.: *Memories*, London, edition of 1914 illus. by Maud Earl.

GARTON, R. V.: *Dogs and Guns*, London, 1964.

GLASS, E.: *The Cocker Spaniel*, Battle Creek, n.d.

GORDON, J. F.: *The Spaniel Owner's Encyclopaedia*, London, 1967. Revised 1978.

HARMAN, I.: *Cocker Spaniels*, London, 1950.

HARMAR, H.: *The Cocker Spaniel*, New York, 1969.

HART, E. H.: *The Cocker Spaniel Handbook*, New Jersey, 1975.

HOWARD, F.: (Earl of Carlisle): *Poems for the Monument of a favourite Spaniel*, London, 1773 *et. seq.*

JACKSON, A.: (ed.) *The Complete Book of Gundogs in Britain*, London, 1974.

JAGDSPANIELKLUB: *Der Jagdspaniel*, Berlin, n.d.

JENKINS, C. C.: *The Cocker Spaniel*, 1983.

JOHNS, R.: *Our Friend the Cocker Spaniel*, London, 1932 *et. seq.*

KRASUCHI, R. M.: *The New Complete Cocker Spaniel*, 1975.

LLOYD, F. E.: *All Spaniels; Their Breaking, Rearing and Training*, New York, 1930.

LLOYD, H. S.: *The Popular Cocker Spaniel*, London, 1924 *et. seq.*

LUCAS-LUCAS, V.: *The Popular Cocker Spaniel*, London, 1963.

MCCARTHY, D.: *The Cocker Spaniel*, n.d.

MERCER, F. H. F.: *The Spaniel and Its Training*, New York, 1890.
   (Includes American and English Standards.)

MOXON, P.: *Gundog Training and Field Trials*, London, 1972 *et. seq.*

PHILLIPS, C. A. and CANE, R. C.: *The Sporting Spaniel*, Manchester, 1906
   et. seq.

RADCLIFF, T.: *Spaniels for Sport.*

VON MURALT, C.: *Die englischen Spaniel oder Stöberhunde*, publ. by
   'Diana', 1897–8.
   Wohner Stammt der Spaniel? Zurich, 1908.
   Der Jagdspaniel, Berlin, 1924.
   Zur Geschichte des Spaniels, Berlin, 1933.

WHITE, K.: *Dog Breeding: A guide to Matings and Breeding.*

WOOLF, V.: *Flush, a Biography*, Edinburgh, 1933.

Index